Teach & Test

Math Grade 4

Table of Contents

How to Use This Book

1. This book can be used in a home or classroom setting. Read through each unit before working with the student(s). Familiarize yourself with the vocabulary and the skills that are introduced at the top of each unit activity page. Use this information as a guide to help instruct the student(s).

2. Choose a quiet place with little or no interruptions (including the telephone). Talk with the student(s) about the purpose of this book and how you will be working as a team to prepare for standardized tests.

3. As an option, copy the unit test and give it as a pretest to identify weak areas.

4. Upon the completion of each unit, you will find a unit test. Discuss the Helping Hand strategy for test taking featured on the test. Use the example on each test as a chance to show the student(s) how to work through a problem and completely fill in the answer circle. Encourage the student(s) to work independently when possible, but this is a learning time and questions should be welcomed. A time limit is given for each test. Instruct the student(s) to use the time allowed efficiently, looking back over the answers if possible. Tell him to continue until he sees the stop sign.

5. Record the score on the record sheet on page 4. If a student has difficulty with any questions, use the cross-reference guide on the inside back cover to identify the skills that need to be reviewed.

Teach & Test

Introduction

Now this makes sense—teaching students the skills and strategies that are expected of them before they are tested!

Many students, parents, and teachers are concerned that standardized test scores do not adequately reflect a child's capabilities. This may be due to one or more of the factors italicized below. The purpose of this book is to reduce the negative impact of these, or similar factors, on a student's standardized test scores. The goal is to target those factors and alter their effects as described.

1. *The student has been taught the tested skills but has forgotten them.* This book is divided into units that are organized similarly to fourth grade textbooks. Instructions for the skill itself are found at the top of each unit activity page, ensuring that the student has been exposed to each key component. The exercises include drill/practice and creative learning activities. Additional activity suggestions can be found in a star burst within the units. These activities require the students to apply the skills that they are practicing.

2. *The student has mastered the skills but has never seen them presented in a test-type format.* Ideally, the skills a student learns at school will be used as part of problem solving in the outside world. For this reason, the skills in this book, and in most classrooms, are not practiced in a test-type format. At the end of each unit in this book, the skills are specifically matched with test questions. In this way, the book serves as a type of "bridge" between the skills that the student(s) has mastered and the standardized test format.

3. *The student is inexperienced with the answer sheet format.* Depending on the standardized test that your school district uses, students are expected to use a fill-in-the-bubble name grid and score sheet. To familiarize students with this process, a name grid and score sheet are included for the review tests found at the midway point and again at the end of the book.

4. *The student may feel the anxiety of a new and unfamiliar situation.* While testing, students will notice changes in their daily routine: their classroom door will be closed with a "Testing" sign on it, children will be asked not to use the restroom, their desks may be separated, their teacher may read from a script and refuse to repeat herself, etc. To help relieve the stress caused by these changes, treat each unit test in this book as it would be treated at school by following the procedures listed below.

Stage a Test

You will find review tests midway through the book and again at the end of the book. When you reach these points, "stage a test" by creating a real test-taking environment. The procedures listed below coincide with many standardized test directions. The purpose is to alleviate stress, rather than contribute to it, so make this a serious, but calm, event and the student(s) will benefit.

1. Prepare! Have the student(s) sharpen two pencils, lay out scratch paper, and use the restroom.

2. Choose a room with a door that can be closed. Ask a student to put a sign on the door that reads "Testing" and explain that no talking will be permitted after the sign is hung.

3. Direct the student(s) to turn to a specific page but not to begin until the instructions are completely given.

4. Read the instructions at the top of the page and work through the example together. Discuss the Helping Hand strategy that is featured at the top of the page. Have the student(s) neatly and completely fill in the bubble for the example. This is the child's last chance to ask for help!

5. Instruct the student(s) to continue working until the stop sign is reached. If a student needs help reading, you may read each question only once.

Helping Hand Test Strategies

The first page of each test features a specific test-taking strategy that will be helpful in working through most standardized tests. These strategies are introduced and spotlighted one at a time so that they will be learned and remembered internally. Each will serve as a valuable test-taking tool, so discuss them thoroughly.

The strategies include:

- Sometimes the correct answer is not given. Fill in the circle beside NG if no answer is correct.
- Always read each question carefully.
- Always read the question twice. Does your answer make sense?
- If you are not sure what the answer is, skip it and come back to it later.
- Cross out answers you know are wrong.
- Read all the answer choices before you choose the one you think is correct.
- Take time to review your answers.
- Note the time allotment. Pace yourself.

Constructed-Response Questions

You will find the final question of each test is written in a different format called constructed response. This means that students are not provided with answer choices, but are instead asked to construct their own answers. The objective of such an "open-ended" type of question is to provide students with a chance to creatively develop reasonable answers. It also provides an insight to a student's reasoning and thinking skills. As this format is becoming more accepted and encouraged by standardized test developers, students will be "ahead of the game" by practicing such responses now.

Evaluating the Tests

Two types of questions are included in each test. The unit tests consist of 20 multiple-choice questions, the midway review test consists of 25 multiple-choice questions, and the final review test consists of 30 multiple-choice questions. All tests include a constructed-response question which requires the student(s) to construct and sometimes support an answer. Use the following procedures to evaluate a student's performance on each test.

1. Use the answer key found on pages 125–128 to correct the tests. Be sure the student(s) neatly and completely filled in the answer circles.

2. Record the scores on the record sheet found on page 4. If the student(s) incorrectly answered any questions, use the cross-reference guide found on the inside back cover to help identify the skills the student(s) needs to review. Each test question references the corresponding activity page.

3. Scoring the constructed-response questions is somewhat subjective. Discuss these questions with the student(s). Sometimes it is easier for the student(s) to explain the answer verbally. Help the student to record his thoughts as a written answer. If the student(s) has difficulty formulating a response, refer back to the activity pages using the cross-reference guide. Also review the star burst activity found in the unit which also requires the student(s) to formulate an answer.

4. Discuss the test with the student(s). What strategies were used to answer the questions? Were some questions more difficult than others? Was there enough time? What strategies did the student(s) use while taking the test?

Record Sheet

Record a student's score for each test by drawing a star or placing a sticker below each item number that was correct. Leave the incorrect boxes empty as this will allow you to visually see any weak spots. Review and practice those missed skills, then retest only the necessary items.

Unit 1

1	2	3	4	5	6	7	8	9	10	11	12	13	14	15	16	17	18	19	20

Unit 2

1	2	3	4	5	6	7	8	9	10	11	12	13	14	15	16	17	18	19	20

Unit 3

1	2	3	4	5	6	7	8	9	10	11	12	13	14	15	16	17	18	19	20

Unit 4

1	2	3	4	5	6	7	8	9	10	11	12	13	14	15	16	17	18	19	20

Midway Review Test

1	2	3	4	5	6	7	8	9	10	11	12	13	14	15	16	17	18	19	20

21	22	23	24	25

Unit 5

1	2	3	4	5	6	7	8	9	10	11	12	13	14	15	16	17	18	19	20

Unit 6

1	2	3	4	5	6	7	8	9	10	11	12	13	14	15	16	17	18	19	20

Unit 7

1	2	3	4	5	6	7	8	9	10	11	12	13	14	15	16	17	18	19	20

Unit 8

1	2	3	4	5	6	7	8	9	10	11	12	13	14	15	16	17	18	19	20

Final Review Test

1	2	3	4	5	6	7	8	9	10	11	12	13	14	15	16	17	18	19	20

21	22	23	24	25	26	27	28	29	30

Name

Using parentheses to learn addition and subtraction facts

Always do the operation inside the parentheses first. Then solve.

Example: $(18 - 10) + 7 = \square$ → $18 - 10 = 8$ → $8 + 7 = \boxed{15}$

Solve the equations.

1. $(4 + 5) + 7 =$ _____   2. $7 + (4 + 5) =$ _____

3. $17 - (3 + 5) =$ _____   4. $11 - (2 + 3) =$ _____

5. $(7 + 7) - 8 =$ _____   6. $13 - (3 + 5) =$ _____

7. $(4 + 6) - 7 =$ _____   8. $(6 + 3) + 8 =$ _____

9. $(18 - 7) + 4 =$ _____   10. $(6 + 7) - 6 =$ _____

11. $5 + (3 + 5) =$ _____   12. $(15 - 7) + 9 =$ _____

13. $(16 - 7) + 4 =$ _____   14. $7 + (10 - 2) =$ _____

15. $(14 - 9) + 7 =$ _____   16. $8 + (6 + 3) =$ _____

17. $7 + (14 - 6) =$ _____   18. $(17 - 9) + 4 =$ _____

19. $(3 + 3) + 8 =$ _____   20. $(20 - 10) + 5 =$ _____

21. $(17 - 8) + 7 =$ _____   22. $(4 + 8) - 7 =$ _____

23. $5 + (15 - 8) =$ _____   24. $13 - (4 + 3) =$ _____

25. $16 - (4 + 5) =$ _____   26. $(8 + 6) - 9 =$ _____

Name

Comparing numbers

The greater than (>) and less than (<) symbols always point to the number of lesser value. Numbers of equal value use the equal sign (=).

Examples:
543 > 53   24 < 359   204 = 204

◯ > ○   ○ < ◯   ◯ = ○

Use the symbols **>**, **<**, and **=** to compare the numbers below.

A. 61 ◯ 60   4,128 ◯ 2,199   2,145 ◯ 8,415

B. 34 ◯ 43   542 ◯ 249   809 ◯ 809

C. 24 ◯ 14   1,215 ◯ 5,187   9,214 ◯ 4,482

D. 351 ◯ 350   51,215 ◯ 51,215   814 ◯ 4,285

E. 921 ◯ 9,219   319,114 ◯ 312,546   312 ◯ 645

F. 48 ◯ 48   5,198 ◯ 426   8,249 ◯ 511

G. 92 ◯ 28   3,291 ◯ 5,982

Compare the year you were born with these numbers: 1,815; 1,995; and 2,075.

H. 432 ◯ 396   5,214 ◯ 6,294

I. 5,218 ◯ 4,329   32,192 ◯ 49,140

Rounding

Unit 1

When rounding a number, always look to the digit to the right of the place to which you are rounding. If that digit is 4 or less, round down. If it is 5 or more, round up.

Examples: Nearest ten: 3**4**   Nearest hundred: 4**87**   Nearest thousand 2,**279**

          3**4**: round down to 30   4**87**: round up to 500   2,**279**: round down to 2,000

Solve the problems. Remember: always look to the right.

Round to the nearest ten.

72 _____   14 _____

83 _____   49 _____

55 _____   62 _____

17 _____   29 _____

34 _____   95 _____

68 _____   41 _____

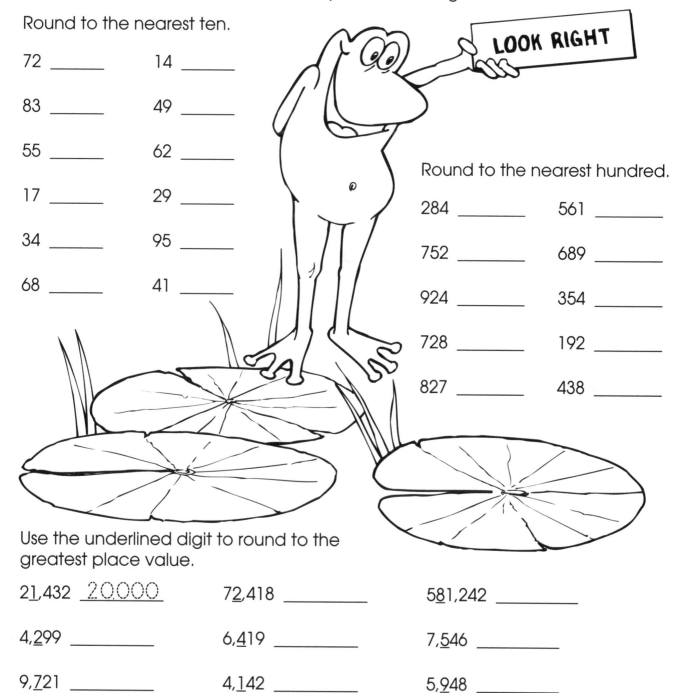

LOOK RIGHT

Round to the nearest hundred.

284 _____   561 _____

752 _____   689 _____

924 _____   354 _____

728 _____   192 _____

827 _____   438 _____

Use the underlined digit to round to the greatest place value.

2_1_,432 _20,000_   7_2_,418 _____   5_8_1,242 _____

4,_2_99 _____   6,_4_19 _____   7,_5_46 _____

9,_7_21 _____   4,_1_42 _____   5,_9_48 _____

3_8_,201 _____   3_4_,112 _____   6,_4_18,205 _____

Name

Addition of two- and three-digit numbers   Unit 1

Add the ones column. Regroup by carrying the tens.

```
    1
  3 2 1
  1 5 7
+   2 4 3
─────────
        1
```

Add the tens column. Regroup by carrying the hundreds.

```
  1 1
  3 2 1
  1 5 7
+   2 4 3
─────────
      2 1
```

Add the hundreds.

```
  1 1
  3 2 1
  1 5 7
+   2 4 3
─────────
    7 2 1
```

Solve the problems.

1.
```
    42
    17
+   34
```

2.
```
    25
    43
+   18
```

3.
```
    72
    43
+   18
```

4.
```
    38
    42
+   17
```

5.
```
    56
    42
+   34
```

6.
```
   463
+  259
```

7.
```
   248
+  367
```

8.
```
   528
+  279
```

9.
```
   382
+  478
```

10.
```
   384
+  297
```

11.
```
   215
   146
+  318
```

12.
```
   623
   168
+  235
```

13.
```
   742
   128
+  296
```

14.
```
   542
   187
+  364
```

15.
```
   523
   146
+  387
```

Solve the problems. Use the code to find the hidden message. Change each digit in the sums into a letter and write the letters in order on the lines below.

1 = T	2 = B	3 = A	4 = H	5 = M	6 = !	7 = I	8 = S	9 = L

```
   247
+  284
```

```
   153
+  325
```

```
     1
+    2
```

```
   106
+  187
```

```
   329
+  487
```

___ ___ ___   ___ ___ ___   ___   ___ ___ ___ ___

Name

Addition of greater numbers

Add the ones. Regroup if necessary.	Add the tens. Regroup if necessary	Add the hundreds. Regroup if necessary.	Add the thousands.
1 3,465 + 2,597 2	1 1 3,465 + 2,597 6 2	1 1 1 3,465 + 2,597 0 6 2	1 1 1 3,465 + 2,597 6,062

Solve the problems.

1.
```
    7,432
+   1,298
```

2.
```
    5,068
+   2,753
```

3.
```
    8,430
+   2,193
```

4.
```
    2,573
+   1,842
```

5.
```
      389
+  64,413
```

6.
```
    4,568
+     978
```

7.
```
   32,146
+  13,927
```

8.
```
   41,387
+   2,176
```

9.
```
   56,143
+   2,478
```

10.
```
   72,615
+  23,827
```

11.
```
   42,516
+  19,827
```

12.
```
   56,247
+  17,085
```

13.
```
   62,148
+  19,382
```

14.
```
   92,416
+  13,592
```

15.
```
  325,146
+  26,328
```

16.
```
  642,158
+  51,319
```

Name

Three- and four-digit subtraction

If necessary, borrow from the tens and regroup. Subtract.

```
    3 13
  2,1 4 8
-   1,8 2 5
─────────
        8
```

```
    3 13
  2,1 4 8
-   1,8 2 5
─────────
       18
```

If necessary, borrow from the thousands and regroup. Subtract.

```
  1 11 3 13
   2,1 4 8
-    1,8 2 5
─────────
       318
```

Solve the problems.

1.
```
    642
-   384
```

2.
```
    549
-   293
```

3.
```
    754
-   628
```

4.
```
    592
-   328
```

5.
```
    462
-   285
```

6.
```
    744
-   256
```

7.
```
  2,143
- 1,385
```

8.
```
  7,469
- 3,873
```

9.
```
  4,685
-   928
```

10.
```
  6,435
- 4,972
```

11.
```
  9,846
-   928
```

12.
```
  3,764
- 1,878
```

13.
```
  5,648
- 3,959
```

14.
```
  4,657
- 2,879
```

15.
```
  8,408
- 6,519
```

16.
```
  7,645
- 3,789
```

Borrow

Subtraction of greater numbers

Borrow from each digit to the left as needed. Regroup. Subtract.

```
                        4 14                 2 14 11 14 14
    35,254          35,2̶5̶4̶              ̶3̶5̶,̶2̶5̶4̶
  -  18,375        -  18,375            -  18,375
                            9              16,879
```

Solve the problems.

1.
```
   3,642
 -  1,896
```

2.
```
   7,261
 -  2,893
```

3.
```
   8,476
 -  2,598
```

4.
```
   7,894
 -  3,958
```

5.
```
  87,145
 -  9,318
```

6.
```
  89,642
 -    984
```

7.
```
  24,318
 -  18,249
```

8.
```
  67,148
 -  29,359
```

9.
```
  37,242
 -  18,139
```

10.
```
  84,286
 -  51,289
```

11.
```
  19,487
 -  13,829
```

12.
```
  58,146
 -  24,898
```

13.
```
  85,274
 -  67,529
```

14.
```
  38,462
 -  19,584
```

15.
```
  74,864
 -  28,481
```

16.
```
  174,242
 -  81,428
```

Name _____

Subtracting with zeroes

Begin at the ones column. You cannot subtract from zero. Seek out the first digit that is one or greater. Borrow. Regroup. Borrow again if necessary. Regroup. Begin subtracting from the ones column.

```
                    3 10          9               9
                                3 10 10         3 10 10
      400           400          400            400
    -  285        -  285       -  285         -  285
                                                  115
```

Borrow   Regroup

Solve the problems.

1.
```
   508
-  142
```

2.
```
   640
-  239
```

3.
```
   250
-  128
```

4.
```
   700
-  124
```

5.
```
   700
-  527
```

6.
```
   808
-  564
```

7.
```
  3,006
- 1,242
```

8.
```
  6,240
- 4,193
```

9.
```
  9,040
- 2,318
```

10.
```
  7,048
- 6,529
```

11.
```
  3,000
-   147
```

12.
```
  9,048
-   329
```

13.
```
  6,408
- 2,299
```

14.
```
  5,000
- 2,084
```

15.
```
  8,405
-   521
```

16.
```
  4,205
-   812
```

Name

Addition and subtraction of money

When adding and subtracting money, always make sure that the decimal point lines up in the problem and also in the sum or difference. Then add or subtract and include the dollar sign ($) in your answer.

$$\begin{array}{r} \$3.42 \\ +\ 1.25 \\ \hline \end{array} \qquad \begin{array}{r} \$2.58 \\ +\ 1.23 \\ \hline \end{array} \qquad \begin{array}{r} \$13.42 \\ +\ 2.81 \\ \hline \end{array}$$

Solve the problems.

LINE UP DECIMAL POINTS

1. $$\begin{array}{r} \$\ .51 \\ +\ \ .92 \\ \hline \end{array}$$

2. $$\begin{array}{r} \$3.45 \\ +\ 4.82 \\ \hline \end{array}$$

3. $$\begin{array}{r} \$41.23 \\ +\ 29.38 \\ \hline \end{array}$$

4. $$\begin{array}{r} \$\ .94 \\ -\ \ .38 \\ \hline \end{array}$$

5. $$\begin{array}{r} \$2.75 \\ -\ 1.82 \\ \hline \end{array}$$

6. $$\begin{array}{r} \$38.41 \\ -\ 19.24 \\ \hline \end{array}$$

7. $$\begin{array}{r} \$423.14 \\ +\ 180.93 \\ \hline \end{array}$$

8. $$\begin{array}{r} \$525.42 \\ +\ 48.29 \\ \hline \end{array}$$

9. $$\begin{array}{r} \$42.91 \\ +\ 318.09 \\ \hline \end{array}$$

10. $$\begin{array}{r} \$301.24 \\ -\ 130.19 \\ \hline \end{array}$$

11. $$\begin{array}{r} \$421.24 \\ -\ 150.82 \\ \hline \end{array}$$

12. $$\begin{array}{r} \$500.27 \\ -\ 123.16 \\ \hline \end{array}$$

Solve each problem. Use the code. Write the letters in order in the blanks below to find out what Billy bought with the money he saved.

1 = E	6 = B
2 = N	7 = W
3 = Y	8 = C
4 = A	9 = I
5 = L	0 = !

$$\begin{array}{r} \$91.70 \\ -\ 49.53 \\ \hline \end{array} \qquad \begin{array}{r} \$80.90 \\ -\ 11.07 \\ \hline \end{array} \qquad \begin{array}{r} \$86.15 \\ -\ 1.05 \\ \hline \end{array}$$

___ ___ ___ ___ ___   ___ ___ ___ ___ ___ ___

Name

Read the question. Use an extra piece of paper to write the problems down and solve them. Fill in the circle beside the best answer.

☐ Example:

Round 468 to the nearest hundred.

Ⓐ 400

Ⓑ 500

Ⓒ 40

Ⓓ NG

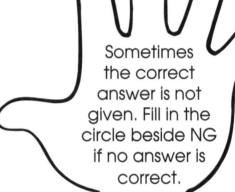

Sometimes the correct answer is not given. Fill in the circle beside NG if no answer is correct.

Answer: B because the 6 in the tens place is 5 or more, so we round up.

Now try these. You have 20 minutes. Continue until you see .

---

1. How many of these problems equal 17?

$12 + (1 + 14) = \square$ $8 + (4 + 5) = \square$

$14 - (3 + 4) = \square$ $20 - (2 + 1) = \square$

Ⓐ 4   Ⓑ 2

Ⓒ 3   Ⓓ NG

---

2. Which symbol makes this number sentence true?

$4{,}258 \bigcirc 428$

Ⓐ >   Ⓑ <

Ⓒ =   Ⓓ NG

---

3. Round 42,198 to the nearest ten thousand.

42,100	40,000	50,000	42,200
Ⓐ	Ⓑ	Ⓒ	Ⓓ

4.

$\begin{array}{r} 5{,}214 \\ -\ 2{,}805 \\ \hline \end{array}$

8,019	4,199	2,409	NG
Ⓐ	Ⓑ	Ⓒ	Ⓓ

GO ON ▷

Name

5.

$248.12
−   71.21

$176.91
(A)

$184.51
(B)

$175.24
(C)

$319.33
(D)

6. How many of these number sentences equal less than 8?

15 − (4 + 3) = ☐   (5 + 8) + 5 = ☐   (A) 3   (B) 1

17 − (5 + 3) = ☐   4 + (8 − 6) = ☐   (C) 4   (D) NG

7.

36
421
+ 382

654
(A)

841
(B)

925
(C)

NG
(D)

8. Round 5,832 to the nearest thousand.

5,000
(A)

7,000
(B)

4,000
(C)

6,000
(D)

9.

4,385
+ 5,924

10,309
(A)

4,199
(B)

12,438
(C)

1,539
(D)

10.

3,005
− 1,243

2,143
(A)

1,540
(B)

1,762
(C)

4,248
(D)

11. Which symbol makes this number sentence true?

523,146 ◯ 523,146

(A) >   (B) <

(C) =   (D) NG

12.

$421.56
+ 358.29

$779.85 Ⓐ $852.49 Ⓑ $924.56 Ⓒ   NG Ⓓ

13.

7,000
- 3,214

4,214 Ⓐ   5,132 Ⓑ   3,786 Ⓒ   10,214 Ⓓ

14. Which number sentences are equal?

A. 13 – (5 + 4) = ☐

B. 3 + (10 – 9) = ☐

C. 14 – (3 + 4) = ☐

Ⓐ B and C

Ⓑ A and B

Ⓒ A, B, and C

Ⓓ NG

15.

321,438
+ 38,162

321,500 Ⓐ   359,600 Ⓑ   400,258 Ⓒ   283,276 Ⓓ

16.

85,241
- 26,190

60,242 Ⓐ   59,000 Ⓑ   48,245 Ⓒ   59,051 Ⓓ

17. Round 642,584 to the nearest hundred thousand.

600,000 Ⓐ   700,000 Ⓑ   640,000 Ⓒ   NG Ⓓ

18. Which symbol makes this number sentence true?

16 – (3 + 4) ◯ 13 + (8 – 2)

Ⓐ >   Ⓑ <

Ⓒ =   Ⓓ NG

GO ON

Unit 1 Test

19. Add. Round the sum to the nearest hundred.

35	100	200	300	NG
29	Ⓐ	Ⓑ	Ⓒ	Ⓓ
+ 46				

20.

38,417	19,240	18,893	11,240	57,941
– 19,524	Ⓐ	Ⓑ	Ⓒ	Ⓓ

Create a story about you and your friends. Write the number sentence that goes along with your story.

Example: 14 – (3 + 4) = ☐

Story: My family and I went on a family vacation to California for 14 days. We spent the first 3 days in San Diego. We spent the next 4 days in Los Angeles. How many days of vacation were left?

_____

_____

_____

_____

_____

Name

Multiplying factors 0–12

Multiplication is a quick way to add.

3 x 8 = ___

Think: 3 "groups of" 8 = ___

3 x 8 = 24

Multiply.

1. 6 x 3	8 x 4	11 x 0	9 x 5	3 x 7
2. 7 x 4	12 x 3	10 x 1	8 x 9	4 x 6
3. 12 x 2	3 x 4	11 x 3	9 x 4	6 x 6
4. 2 x 7	11 x 2	5 x 5	8 x 7	11 x 6
5. 12 x 0	4 x 4	6 x 7	7 x 7	12 x 8

A QUICK WAY TO ADD

Complete the multiplication paragraph below.

I ____ be ____ I came over ____ night. My steak was very ____ der and
2 x 4   1 x 4   1 x 2   2 x 5

delicious, ____! ____ many people pre____d ____ be full. Of____ they are
2 x 1   1 x 2   5 x 2   1 x 2   2 x 5

____ding ____ other things and ____ get ____ eat! No ____der they
5 x 2   1 x 2   2 x 2   1 x 2   1 x 1

____d ____ be hungry when they say they have already ea____!
5 x 2   2 x 1   2 x 5

Name

Multiplying 2-digit numbers

Unit 2

Multiply the ones column.
Place the ones and regroup the tens.
6 x 9 = 54 (5 tens and 4 ones)

```
    5
   89
x    6
    4
```

Multiply the tens column.
Add the 5 tens. 6 x 8 tens = 48 tens
48 tens + 5 tens = 53 tens

```
    5
   89
x    6
  534
```

Multiply.

1.
```
   23
x   3
```

2.
```
   24
x   4
```

3.
```
   42
x   2
```

4.
```
   10
x   7
```

5.
```
   18
x   5
```

6.
```
   21
x   9
```

7.
```
   92
x   3
```

8.
```
   41
x   6
```

9.
```
   62
x   4
```

10.
```
   90
x   9
```

11.
```
   62
x   7
```

12.
```
   32
x   5
```

13.
```
   35
x   8
```

14.
```
   47
x   3
```

15.
```
   38
x   5
```

16.
```
   25
x   6
```

17.
```
   23
x   9
```

18.
```
   46
x   3
```

19.
```
   64
x   4
```

20.
```
   87
x   3
```

Multiplying 3-digit numbers

Multiply the ones.
Regroup the tens.
3 x 9 = 27 (2 tens and 7 ones)

```
    2
  279
x   3
    7
```

Multiply the tens. 3 x 7 = 21
Add the 2 tens. 21 + 2 = 23
Regroup the hundreds.

```
  2 2
  279
x   3
   37
```

Multiply the hundreds. 3 x 2 = 6
Add the 2 hundreds. 6 + 2 = 8

```
  2 2
  279
x   3
  837
```

Multiply.

1.
```
  214
x   3
```

2.
```
  284
x   2
```

3.
```
  510
x   5
```

4.
```
  243
x   4
```

5.
```
  131
x   8
```

6.
```
  123
x   6
```

7.
```
  514
x   4
```

8.
```
  213
x   7
```

9.
```
  412
x   9
```

10.
```
  842
x   3
```

11.
```
  354
x   5
```

12.
```
  126
x   8
```

13.
```
  408
x   6
```

14.
```
  237
x   3
```

15.
```
  543
x   4
```

3-digit

Multiplying 4-digit numbers

Multiply the ones.	Multiply the tens. $6 \times 3 = 18$	Multiply the hundreds.	Multiply the
$6 \times 8 = 48$	Add the 4 tens. $18 + 4 = 22$	$6 \times 2 = 12$	thousands.
(4 tens and 8 ones)	Regroup the hundreds.	Add the 2 hundreds.	$6 \times 4 = 24$
Regroup the tens.		$12 + 2 = 14$	Add the 1 thousand.
		Regroup the thousands.	$24 + 1 = 25$

```
      4                 2 4                1 2 4              1 2 4
  4,238             4,238              4,238              4,238
x       6         x       6          x       6          x       6
_____          _____           _____           _____
      8                28                428             25,428
```

Multiply.

1.
```
  3,123
x     3
```

2.
```
  4,243
x     2
```

3.
```
  4,321
x     6
```

4.
```
  1,228
x     4
```

5.
```
  2,752
x     4
```

6.
```
  4,523
x     5
```

7.
```
  8,463
x     2
```

8.
```
  8,427
x     3
```

9.
```
  5,139
x     6
```

10.
```
  4,687
x     3
```

11.
```
  2,314
x     8
```

12.
```
  4,613
x     7
```

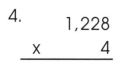 Write a multiplication problem that only uses regrouping from tens to hundreds.

Name

Multiplying by tens, hundreds, and thousands

Unit 2

When multiplying by these numbers, begin by multiplying the factors other than zero.
Next, simply add the number of zeroes in the problem to the product.

3000 x 3	Multiply the factors other than zero.	3 x 3 9	Add the zeroes in the problem to the product.

3000
x   3
9,000

Multiply.

1.   300
   x   6

2.   400
   x   7

3.   800
   x   5

4.   240
   x   2

5.   50
   x   4

6.   200
   x   9

7.   80
   x   3

8.   60
   x   4

9.   8,000
   x   4

10.   7,000
    x   6

11.   400
    x   8

12.   2,000
    x   6

13.   8,000
    x   6

14.   3,200
    x   3

15.   20
    x   10

16.   40
    x   30

17.   80
    x   20

18.   100
    x   70

19.   200
    x   40

20.   800
    x   10

Name

Multiplying by 2-digit numbers   Unit 2

Multiply by the ones digit.		Place a zero in the ones column. Multiply by the tens digit.		Add.	
	2 28 x 63 84		4 2̸ 28 x 63 84 + 1,680		4 2̸ 28 x 63 84 + 1,680 1,764

Multiply.

1.   21
    x   32

2.   22
    x   42

3.   27
    x   38

4.   57
    x   48

5.   23
    x   53

6.   23
    x   45

7.   25
    x   61

8.   28
    x   47

9.   28
    x   19

10.   69
    x   34

11.   36
    x   72

12.   13
    x   82

13.   28
    x   49

14.   89
    x   14

Name

Multiplying 3-digit numbers by 2-digit numbers

Multiply by the ones digit.

```
    3 3
    378
x    34
   1512
```

Place a zero in the ones column. Multiply by the tens digit.

```
    2 2
    3̶ 3̶
    378
x    34
   1512
+ 11340
```

Add.

```
    2 2
    3̶ 3̶
    378
x    34
   1512
+ 11340
  12,852
```

Multiply.

1.
```
  310
x  24
```

2.
```
  412
x  35
```

3.
```
  362
x  28
```

4.
```
  420
x  41
```

5.
```
  543
x  23
```

6.
```
  246
x  51
```

7.
```
  185
x  43
```

8.
```
  324
x  81
```

9.
```
  624
x  27
```

10.
```
  846
x  34
```

11.
```
  231
x  55
```

12.
```
  418
x  23
```

Name

Multiplication of money   Unit 2

Multiply.

$$
\begin{array}{r}
\overset{2}{\cancel{1}} \\
\$3.51 \\
\times \quad 42 \\
\hline
702 \\
+ \quad 14040 \\
\hline
14742
\end{array}
$$

Add the dollar ($) sign and decimal point (.). When working with money, the decimal point goes before the second digit from the right.

$$
\begin{array}{r}
\overset{2}{\cancel{1}} \\
\$3.51 \\
\times \quad 42 \\
\hline
702 \\
+ \quad 14040 \\
\hline
\$147.42
\end{array}
$$

Multiply. Do not forget to add the dollar sign and the decimal point.

1. $2.41
    x   23

2. $3.89
    x   6

3. $ .21
    x   34

4. $24.12
    x   8

5. $ .84
    x   31

6. $15.41
    x   3

7. $9.25
    x   34

8. $.74
    x   51

9. $ .49
    x   21

10. $ 4.21
     x   7

11. $3.24
     x   14

12. $8.54
     x   16

13. $2.12
     x   42

14. $ .13
     x   92

Estimation

Round each factor to its greatest place value.	Estimate by using mental computation.	Check your answer and compare.	Are both answers close?
$4.92 x 36 = $5 x 40	$5 x 40 $200	$4.92 x 36 $177.12	Estimate: $200 Real: $177.12 Yes, it's accurate!

Solve the problems. Do the second problem first. If both products are close, your answer is probably correct.

1.
$3.41
x   6
=
$3
x   6

2.
$ .41
x   24
=
x _____

3.
$9.87
x   8
=
x _____

4.
$4.69
x   21
=
x _____

Take a guess at the prices of these items. Find each product to discover the real price.

5.

SALTED PEANUTS $3.41
Box of 50

Guess: _____

$3.41
x   50

Real Price: _____

6.
$2.72
Box of 15

Guess: _____

$2.72
x   15

Real Price: _____

7.
$12.41
Box of 8

Guess: _____

$12.41
x   8

Real Price: _____

Name

Read the question. Use an extra piece of paper to write problems down and solve them.
Fill in the circle beside the best answer.

☐ Example:

What is the missing factor?

$$\begin{array}{r} 9{,}000 \\ \times 3 \\ \hline \end{array}$$

(A) 270

(B) 2,700

(C) 27,000

(D) NG

Always read each question carefully.

Answer: C because 3 x 9 = 27. Then you add 3 zeroes to get 27,000.

Now try these. You have 20 minutes. Continue until you see .

1.

$$\begin{array}{r} 49 \\ \times 23 \\ \hline \end{array}$$

1,127 (A)

1,248 (B)

2,327 (C)

1,437 (D)

---

2. What is wrong with this problem?

$$\begin{array}{r} 11 \\ \cancel{12} \\ 135 \\ \times 35 \\ \hline 675 \\ 405 \\ \hline 1{,}080 \end{array}$$

(A) regrouping digits not crossed out

(B) zero missing in beginning of second row to signify multiplication of tens

(C) factors multiplied incorrectly

(D) NG

3.

$$\begin{array}{r} \$4.21 \\ \times 8 \\ \hline \end{array}$$

$29.40 (A)

$33.69 (B)

$41.32 (C)

$33.68 (D)

GO ON

4. Which of these problems does not equal 24?

4 x 6	2 x 12	5 x 6	NG
Ⓐ	Ⓑ	Ⓒ	Ⓓ

5. Which statement about this problem is incorrect?

$$\begin{array}{r} \$8.34 \\ \times \quad 31 \\ \hline \end{array}$$

Ⓐ The problem estimate is 9 x 40.

Ⓑ The product estimate is $240.

Ⓒ The actual product is less than $300.00.

Ⓓ The product estimate is less than the actual product.

6.

$$\begin{array}{r} 3,612 \\ \times \quad 9 \\ \hline \end{array}$$

35,214	32,508	42,818	32,805
Ⓐ	Ⓑ	Ⓒ	Ⓓ

7.

$$\begin{array}{r} 4,000 \\ \times \quad 6 \\ \hline \end{array}$$

26,000	30,000	24,000	10,000
Ⓐ	Ⓑ	Ⓒ	Ⓓ

8.

$$\begin{array}{r} 89 \\ \times \quad 5 \\ \hline \end{array}$$

445	521	890	NG
Ⓐ	Ⓑ	Ⓒ	Ⓓ

9.

$$\begin{array}{r} 249 \\ \times \quad 6 \\ \hline \end{array}$$

1,244	1,494	1,294	1,444
Ⓐ	Ⓑ	Ⓒ	Ⓓ

10.

$$\begin{array}{r} 149 \\ \times \quad 25 \\ \hline \end{array}$$

3,724	4,741	3,720	3,725
Ⓐ	Ⓑ	Ⓒ	Ⓓ

GO ON

Unit 2 Test

---

11. How many zeroes will there be in the product?

$$\begin{array}{r} 700 \\ \times \quad 30 \\ \hline \end{array}$$

5
Ⓐ

7
Ⓑ

3
Ⓒ

NG
Ⓓ

---

12. How many products are greater than 50?

$6 \times 6 = \square$ $7 \times 7 = \square$

$6 \times 9 = \square$ $8 \times 10 = \square$

Ⓐ 3   Ⓑ 4

Ⓒ 1   Ⓓ NG

13.

$$\begin{array}{r} 409 \\ \times \quad 23 \\ \hline \end{array}$$

9,003
Ⓐ

8,249
Ⓑ

9,407
Ⓒ

9,704
Ⓓ

---

14. What is wrong with this problem?

$$\begin{array}{r} \$23.48 \\ \times \qquad 9 \\ \hline \$21.132 \end{array}$$

Ⓐ incorrect multiplying

Ⓑ decimal point is in wrong place

Ⓒ mistake in regrouping

Ⓓ mistake not given

15.

$$\begin{array}{r} 89 \\ \times \quad 64 \\ \hline \end{array}$$

5,690
Ⓐ

6,594
Ⓑ

5,696
Ⓒ

890
Ⓓ

---

16. Which is the correct rounded estimate?

$$\begin{array}{r} \$9.28 \\ \times \qquad 27 \\ \hline \end{array}$$

30 x 8
Ⓐ

20 x 10
Ⓑ

30 x 9
Ⓒ

20 x 9
Ⓓ

GO ON

17.

$$\begin{array}{r} 2{,}154 \\ \times \quad 9 \end{array}$$

19,386
(A)

21,214
(B)

18,482
(C)

19,885
(D)

18. What is the missing regrouped digit?

$$\begin{array}{r} 59 \\ \times \quad 3 \end{array}$$

3
(A)

2
(B)

4
(C)

NG
(D)

19. If you buy 4 bags of pretzels, how much will you spend?

$3.50
(A)

$4.89
(B)

$3.56
(C)

$3.80
(D)

20.

$$\begin{array}{r} 842 \\ \times \quad 29 \end{array}$$

24,418
(A)

29,318
(B)

40,408
(C)

9,262
(D)

Take a pretend trip to a department store. Purchase 4 of the same item with a price over $20.00. How much is the item, and how much will you spend? Show your work.

STOP

Name

1-digit quotients with remainders

Is the tens digit great enough to divide into? No. We must divide into the 51 ones.	How many groups of 7 come closest to equaling 51? 7	Multiply the partial quotient (7) by the divisor (7) and subtract the product (49) from the dividend.	Is the difference great enough to divide into? No. It becomes the remainder.

$$7\overline{)51}$$

$$7$$
$$7\overline{)51}$$

$$7$$
$$7\overline{)51}$$
$$-49$$
$$\overline{2}$$

$$7\text{ R2}$$
$$7\overline{)51}$$
$$-49$$
$$\overline{2}$$

Divide.

1. $5\overline{)27}$ 2. $2\overline{)17}$ 3. $6\overline{)25}$ 4. $7\overline{)23}$

5. $4\overline{)19}$ 6. $9\overline{)84}$ 7. $6\overline{)39}$ 8. $8\overline{)20}$

9. $5\overline{)48}$ 10. $9\overline{)30}$ 11. $6\overline{)35}$ 12. $4\overline{)35}$

13. $5\overline{)19}$ 14. $9\overline{)50}$ 15. $7\overline{)44}$ 16. $3\overline{)17}$

17. $6\overline{)15}$ 18. $8\overline{)44}$ 19. $4\overline{)23}$ 20. $8\overline{)75}$

Name

2-digit quotients—no remainders Unit 3

Is the tens digit great enough to divide into? Yes. Divide. Multiply the partial quotient by the divisor and subtract.

$$\begin{array}{r} 1 \\ 3\overline{)42} \\ -3 \\ \hline 1 \end{array}$$

Is the difference of 1 great enough to divide into? No. Bring down the 2 ones. You now have 12 ones.

$$\begin{array}{r} 1 \\ 3\overline{)42} \\ -3 \\ \hline 12 \end{array}$$

Is this number great enough to divide into? Yes. Divide. Multiply the partial quotient by the divisor and subtract.

$$\begin{array}{r} 14 \\ 3\overline{)42} \\ -3 \\ \hline 12 \\ -12 \\ \hline 0 \end{array}$$

note: Never write R0. It is understood that there is no remainder when it is left blank.

Divide.

1. $4\overline{)84}$ 2. $3\overline{)96}$ 3. $3\overline{)63}$

4. $2\overline{)68}$ 5. $6\overline{)78}$ 6. $5\overline{)90}$

7. $3\overline{)75}$ 8. $5\overline{)65}$ 9. $3\overline{)51}$ 10. $7\overline{)84}$ 11. $4\overline{)64}$

12. $2\overline{)56}$ 13. $4\overline{)76}$ 14. $6\overline{)72}$ 15. $8\overline{)96}$ 16. $2\overline{)76}$

2-digit quotients with remainders   Unit 3

Is the tens digit great enough to divide into? Yes. Divide. Multiply the partial quotient by the divisor and subtract.

Is the difference of 1 great enough to divide into? No. Bring down the 7. Now you have 17 ones.

Is 17 ones great enough to divide into? Yes. Divide. Multiply the partial quotient by the divisor and subtract.

Is the difference of 1 great enough to divide into? No. Are there any more digits in the dividend to bring down? No. The difference becomes a remainder.

```
      1                    1                   14                 14 R1
 4 ) 57               4 ) 57              4 ) 57             4 ) 57
  - 4                  - 4                 - 4                - 4
      1                   17                  17                 17
                                           - 16               - 16
                                              1                  1
```

Divide.

1. 3) 41   2. 5) 59   3. 2) 71   4. 7) 80   5. 4) 91

6. 4) 89   7. 2) 93   8. 3) 47   9. 8) 98   10. 6) 79

11. 5) 79   12. 7) 95   13. 4) 95   14. 5) 72   15. 4) 47

 Write two different division problems which both have a remainder of six.

Name

3-digit quotients—no remainders

Is the hundreds digit great enough to divide into? Yes. Divide. Multiply the partial quotient by the divisor and subtract.

```
      2
  ┌─────
3 │ 852
  − 6
  ─────
      2
```

Is the difference of 2 great enough to divide into? No. Bring down the 5 tens. Now you have 25 tens.

```
      2
  ┌─────
3 │ 852
  − 6
  ─────
     25
```

Divide the 25 tens by the divisor. Multiply and subtract.

```
     28
  ┌─────
3 │ 852
  − 6
  ─────
     25
   − 24
  ─────
      1
```

Is the difference of 1 great enough to divide into? No. Bring down the 2 ones. You now have 12 ones. Divide. Multiply and subtract.

```
    284
  ┌─────
3 │ 852
  − 6
  ─────
     25
   − 24
  ─────
     12
   − 12
  ─────
      0
```

Divide.

1. 3) 435   2. 6) 822   3. 5) 645   4. 2) 944   5. 8) 984

6. 6) 816   7. 3) 942   8. 4) 872   9. 7) 875   10. 5) 890

11. 7) 945   12. 3) 777   13. 6) 828   14. 4) 588   15. 4) 712

3-digit quotients with remainders

Is the hundreds digit great enough to divide into? Yes. Divide. Multiply the partial quotient by the divisor and subtract.	Is the difference of 1 great enough to divide into? No. Bring down the 6 tens. Divide. Multiply and subtract.	Is the difference of 1 great enough to divide into? No. Bring down the 4 ones. Divide. Multiply and subtract.	Is the difference of 2 great enough to divide into? No. Are there any more digits to bring down in the dividend? No. The 2 becomes a remainder.

```
        2              25              254             254 R2
  3 ) 764        3 ) 764         3 ) 852         3 ) 852
   -  6           -  6            -  6            -  6
      1             16              16              16
                  - 15            - 15            - 15
                     1              14              14
                                  - 12            - 12
                                     2               2
```

Divide.

1. $3 \overline{)536}$ 2. $5 \overline{)728}$ 3. $4 \overline{)874}$ 4. $5 \overline{)643}$ 5. $2 \overline{)695}$

6. $4 \overline{)678}$ 7. $3 \overline{)779}$ 8. $2 \overline{)965}$ 9. $7 \overline{)695}$ 10. $6 \overline{)760}$

11. $7 \overline{)941}$ 12. $6 \overline{)916}$ 13. $5 \overline{)629}$ 14. $2 \overline{)775}$ 15. $8 \overline{)940}$

Zeroes in the quotient

Is the hundreds digit great enough to divide into? Yes. Divide. Multiply and subtract.

```
   2
3 ) 871
  - 6
    2
```

Is the difference of 2 great enough to divide into? No. Bring down the 7. Divide. Multiply and subtract.

```
   29
3 ) 871
  - 6
    27
  - 27
     0
```

Is 0 great enough to divide into? No. Bring down the 1. It is still not enough to divide into. _Place a zero in the quotient._

```
   290
3 ) 871
  - 6
    27
  - 27
    01
  -  0
     1
```

Is the difference of 1 great enough to divide into? No. Are there any more digits to bring down in the dividend? No. Then 1 becomes a remainder.

```
   290 R1
3 ) 871
  - 6
    27
  - 27
    01
  -  0
     1
```

Divide.

1. $3 \overline{)925}$ 2. $5 \overline{)904}$ 3. $2 \overline{)813}$ 4. $4 \overline{)839}$ 5. $7 \overline{)985}$

6. $6 \overline{)656}$ 7. $8 \overline{)966}$ 8. $4 \overline{)434}$ 9. $2 \overline{)680}$ 10. $4 \overline{)760}$

11. $2 \overline{)811}$ 12. $5 \overline{)519}$ 13. $6 \overline{)845}$ 14. $3 \overline{)622}$ 15. $6 \overline{)641}$

Name

3- and 4-digit quotients—no remainders

Is the thousands digit great enough to divide into? No. Divide into the 39 hundreds. Multiply and subtract.

$$\begin{array}{r} 9 \\ 4\,\overline{)3{,}948} \\ -36 \\ \hline 3 \end{array}$$

Is the difference of 3 great enough to divide into? No. Bring down the 4. Divide. Multiply and subtract.

$$\begin{array}{r} 98 \\ 4\,\overline{)3{,}948} \\ -36 \\ \hline 34 \\ -32 \\ \hline 2 \end{array}$$

Is the difference of 2 great enough to divide into? No. Bring down the 8. Divide. Multiply and subtract.

$$\begin{array}{r} 987 \\ 4\,\overline{)3{,}948} \\ -36 \\ \hline 34 \\ -32 \\ \hline 28 \\ -28 \\ \hline 0 \end{array}$$

Check your answer! Multiply the quotient by the divisor. If the product matches your dividend, your answer is correct.

$$\begin{array}{r} 987 \\ \times\quad 4 \\ \hline 3{,}948 \end{array}$$

Divide.

1. $5\,\overline{)4{,}065}$

2. $3\,\overline{)9{,}636}$

3. $2\,\overline{)1{,}968}$

4. $4\,\overline{)5{,}032}$

5. $6\,\overline{)5{,}202}$

6. $4\,\overline{)2{,}560}$

7. $6\,\overline{)5{,}112}$

8. $3\,\overline{)1{,}485}$

9. $9\,\overline{)4{,}923}$

10. $6\,\overline{)3{,}156}$

11. $8\,\overline{)1{,}584}$

12. $4\,\overline{)4{,}980}$

37

Teach & Test Math: Grade 4

Name

3- and 4-digit quotients with remainders   Unit 3

Is the thousands digit great enough to divide into? No. Divide into the 27 hundreds. Multiply and subtract.

```
       6
  4 ) 2,758
   - 2 4
       3
```

Is the difference great enough to divide into? No. Bring down the 5. Divide. Multiply and subtract.

```
      68
  4 ) 2,758
   - 2 4
      35
    - 32
       3
```

Is the difference great enough to divide into? No. Bring down the 8. Divide. Multiply and subtract.

```
     689
  4 ) 2,758
   - 2 4
      35
    - 32
      38
    - 36
       2
```

Is the difference great enough to divide into? No. Are there any more digits in the dividend to carry down? No. The 2 becomes the remainder.

```
     689 R2
  4 ) 2,758
   - 2 4
      35
    - 32
      38
    - 36
       2
```

Divide.

1. 3) 1,286

2. 2) 6,843

3. 5) 1,423

4. 4) 867

5. 6) 2,475

6. 5) 3,174

7. 4) 1,543

8. 3) 9,367

9. 8) 3,618

10. 7) 1,730

11. 2) 8,469

12. 6) 2,806

Dividing money

Place the dollar sign and the decimal point in the quotient.

$$\begin{array}{r} \$\ . \\ 3\overline{)\ \$6.48} \end{array}$$

Is the digit in the dollar's place great enough to divide into? Yes. Divide. Multiply and subtract.

$$\begin{array}{r} \$2. \\ 3\overline{)\ \$6.48} \\ -6 \\ \hline 0 \end{array}$$

Is the difference great enough to divide into? No. Bring down the 4. Divide. Multiply and subtract.

$$\begin{array}{r} \$2.1 \\ 3\overline{)\ \$6.48} \\ -6 \\ \hline 04 \\ -3 \\ \hline 1 \end{array}$$

Is the difference great enough to divide into? No. Bring down the 8. Multiply and subtract.

$$\begin{array}{r} \$2.16 \\ 3\overline{)\ \$6.48} \\ -6 \\ \hline 04 \\ -3 \\ \hline 18 \\ -18 \\ \hline 0 \end{array}$$

Divide.

1. $2\overline{)\ \$6.48}$

2. $3\overline{)\ \$9.69}$

3. $5\overline{)\ \$6.35}$

4. $8\overline{)\ \$9.12}$

5. $4\overline{)\ \$8.64}$

6. $4\overline{)\ \$8.72}$

7. $7\overline{)\ \$7.91}$

8. $4\overline{)\ \$9.44}$

9. $6\overline{)\ \$6.48}$

10. $7\overline{)\ \$8.68}$

11. $4\overline{)\ \$8.76}$

12. $5\overline{)\ \$9.20}$

2-digit divisors with remainders

Is the hundreds digit great enough to divide into? No. The 13 tens? No. So we must divide into the 137 ones.

$$21 \overline{)137}$$

How many groups of 21 are there in 137? Round the divisor to 20. Think: There are five 20s in 100. There is one more in 37. So the partial quotient must be 6.

$$\begin{array}{r} 5 \\ 20 \overline{)100} \\ -100 \\ \hline 0 \end{array} \qquad \begin{array}{r} 1 \\ 20 \overline{)37} \\ -20 \\ \hline 17 \end{array}$$

$$5 + 1 = 6$$

Think about rounding the divisor to predict the amount of the partial quotient.

Divide. Multiply and subtract. Is the difference less than the divisor? Yes. Go on.

$$\begin{array}{r} 6 \\ 21 \overline{)137} \\ -126 \\ \hline 11 \end{array}$$

Is the difference of 11 great enough to divide into? No. So 11 becomes the remainder.

$$\begin{array}{r} 6 \text{ R11} \\ 21 \overline{)137} \\ -126 \\ \hline 11 \end{array}$$

Note: The remainder can be any amount, as long as it is less than the divisor (in this case 21).

Divide.

1. $17 \overline{)54}$ 2. $32 \overline{)130}$ 3. $41 \overline{)215}$ 4. $11 \overline{)106}$ 5. $22 \overline{)180}$

6. $49 \overline{)190}$ 7. $39 \overline{)244}$ 8. $52 \overline{)436}$ 9. $19 \overline{)80}$ 10. $61 \overline{)500}$

11. $31 \overline{)150}$ 12. $78 \overline{)399}$ 13. $81 \overline{)161}$ 14. $29 \overline{)223}$ 15. $13 \overline{)75}$

Unit 3 Test

Division

Read the question. Use an extra piece of paper to write problems down and solve them. Fill in the circle beside the best answer.

☐ Example:

What is wrong with this problem?

$$\begin{array}{r} 4\ 7\ R2 \\ 3\overline{)143} \\ -\ 12 \\ \hline 23 \\ -\ 21 \\ \hline 2 \end{array}$$

Ⓐ The partial quotient should be placed over the 4 in the dividend, not the 1.

Ⓑ The remainder is missing.

Ⓒ The subtraction is incorrect.

Ⓓ NG

Always read the question twice. Does your answer make sense?

Answer: A because you are dividing 14 tens, not 1 hundred.

Now try these. You have 20 minutes. Continue until you see ⟨STOP⟩.

---

1. What is the remainder?

$$\begin{array}{r} 4 \\ 4\overline{)17} \end{array}$$

R3	R1	R6	R2
Ⓐ	Ⓑ	Ⓒ	Ⓓ

2.

$$3\overline{)159}$$

72	61	53	55
Ⓐ	Ⓑ	Ⓒ	Ⓓ

---

3. What is wrong with this problem?

$$\begin{array}{r} 348 \\ 5\overline{)\$17.40} \\ -\ 15 \\ \hline 24 \\ -\ 20 \\ \hline 40 \\ -\ 40 \\ \hline 0 \end{array}$$

Ⓐ The quotient is incorrect.

Ⓑ The remainder is missing.

Ⓒ The dollar sign and decimal point are missing in the quotient.

Ⓓ NG

GO ON ▷

4.

$3\overline{)\$8.07}$

$3.14 (A) $2.69 (B) $5.19 (C)   NG (D)

5.

$4\overline{)1{,}404}$

351 (A)   421 (B)   644 (C)   315 (D)

6.

$4\overline{)107}$

27 R1 (A)   25 R4 (B)   26 R3 (C)   25 R5 (D)

7. What is wrong with this problem?

```
      687 R0
 4 ) 2,748
    - 24
      34
    - 32
      28
    - 28
       0
```

(A) There is an error in the multiplication.

(B) The quotient is incorrect.

(C) Never write "R0". It is understood that there is no remainder when you leave it blank.

(D) NG

8.

$5\overline{)540}$

125 (A)   108 (B)   342 (C)   115 (D)

9.

$6\overline{)52}$

8 R1 (A)   7 R (B)   9 R1 (C)   NG (D)

10. To estimate the quotient, what should you mentally round the divisor to?

$32\overline{)155}$

30 (A)   40 (B)   200 (C)   35 (D)

GO ON

11.

$3 \overline{)9,640}$

4,213 R1
Ⓐ

8,142 R2
Ⓑ

3,213 R1
Ⓒ

4,119 R1
Ⓓ

---

12. What is the missing digit?

$$\begin{array}{r} 8\square9 \\ 2\overline{)1618} \\ -16 \\ \hline 018 \\ -18 \\ \hline 0 \end{array}$$

Ⓐ 8

Ⓑ 4

Ⓒ 0

Ⓓ NG

13.

$3 \overline{)\$8.67}$

$2.46
Ⓐ

$2.89
Ⓑ

$3.48
Ⓒ

$2.98
Ⓓ

14.

$21 \overline{)126}$

8
Ⓐ

4
Ⓑ

7
Ⓒ

NG
Ⓓ

15.

$6 \overline{)84}$

14
Ⓐ

28
Ⓑ

16
Ⓒ

22
Ⓓ

16.

$4 \overline{)634}$

134 R3
Ⓐ

206 R1
Ⓑ

158 R2
Ⓒ

NG
Ⓓ

17.

$4 \overline{)2,348}$

587
Ⓐ

464
Ⓑ

742
Ⓒ

161 R1
Ⓓ

GO ON

18. Which problem has placed the "0" correctly in the quotient.

$$4\overline{)436} = 190$$
(A)

$$5\overline{)535} = 017$$
(B)

$$3\overline{)627} = 209$$
(C)

None are correct.
(D)

19.

$$7\overline{)398}$$

56
(A)

64 R3
(B)

58 R9
(C)

56 R6
(D)

20.

$$54\overline{)110}$$

3 R4
(A)

2 R2
(B)

5 R40
(C)

NG
(D)

Explain why you need a "0" in the quotient in this problem.

$$3\overline{)918}$$

_____

_____

_____

_____

_____

_____

STOP

Tenths

$1 \frac{6}{10}$

What portion of
this box is shaded?

one whole box

What portion of this
box is shaded?

six tenths of a box

Altogether: 1.6
(one and six tenths)

Or you can say:
"One point six," or
"one and six tenths."

1 . 6
one . six tenths

Another Example:

Fraction: $\frac{3}{10}$

Decimal: 0.3

When there are no
whole numbers, place
a "0" in the ones
place, just left of the
decimal point.

0 . 3
no ones . three tenths

Identify. Write as a fraction and a decimal.

1. Fraction: _____

   Decimal: _____

2. Fraction: _____

   Decimal: _____

3. Fraction: _____

   Decimal: _____

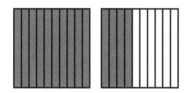

4. Fraction: _____

   Decimal: _____

5. Fraction: _____

   Decimal: _____

6. Fraction: _____

   Decimal: _____

Name

Hundredths

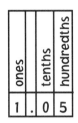

$1 \frac{5}{100}$

What portion of this box is shaded?

one whole box

What portion of this box is shaded?

5 hundredths of a box

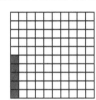

Altogether: 1.05
(one and five hundredths)

1 . 05
_____
one . no tenths five hundredths

Identify. Write as a fraction and a decimal.

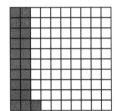 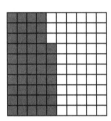 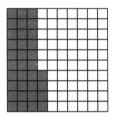 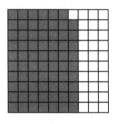

1. Fraction: _____   2. Fraction: _____   3. Fraction: _____   4. Fraction: _____

   Decimal: _____   Decimal: _____   Decimal: _____   Decimal: _____

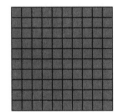   

5. Fraction: _____   6. Fraction: _____

   Decimal: _____   Decimal: _____

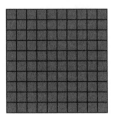 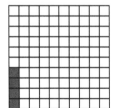 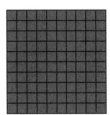   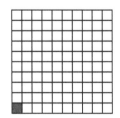

7. Fraction: _____   8. Fraction: _____

   Decimal: _____   Decimal: _____

Teach & Test Math: Grade 4

Name

Comparing decimals   Unit 4

When comparing decimals, if more of a portion is shaded, this is the greater number.

Tenths   Hundredths

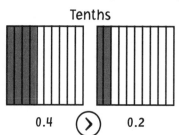   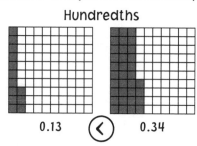

0.4 ⊘ 0.2   0.13 ⓒ 0.34

Another strategy is to compare the digits in the tenths columns.
0.8 > 0.5

If the digits in the tenths columns are the same, compare the digits in the hundredths columns.
0.63 < 0.69

Compare using **>** or **<**.

1. 0.6 ◯ 0.4   2. 0.1 ◯ 0.5   3. 0.23 ◯ 0.03   4. 0.6 ◯ 0.9

5. 0.06 ◯ 0.60   6. 0.4 ◯ 0.7   7. 0.9 ◯ 0.5   8. 0.7 ◯ 0.6

9. 0.42 ◯ 0.14   10. 0.72 ◯ 0.27   11. 0.25 ◯ 0.52   12. 0.7 ◯ 0.3

13. 1.4 ◯ 1.6   14. 3.5 ◯ 3.7   15. 16.2 ◯ 16.8   16. 5.21 ◯ 5.38

17. 2.48 ◯ 2.35   18. 14.5 ◯ 14.3   19. 42.6 ◯ 42.3   20. 3.8 ◯ 3.9

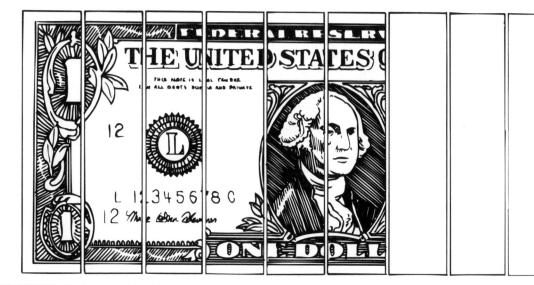

Name

Ordering decimals

To order decimals, start with the number right after the decimal.

Order each set of decimals from least to greatest. The * starts a new set.
Example: 0.1, 0.2, 0.3, 0.4, 0.5

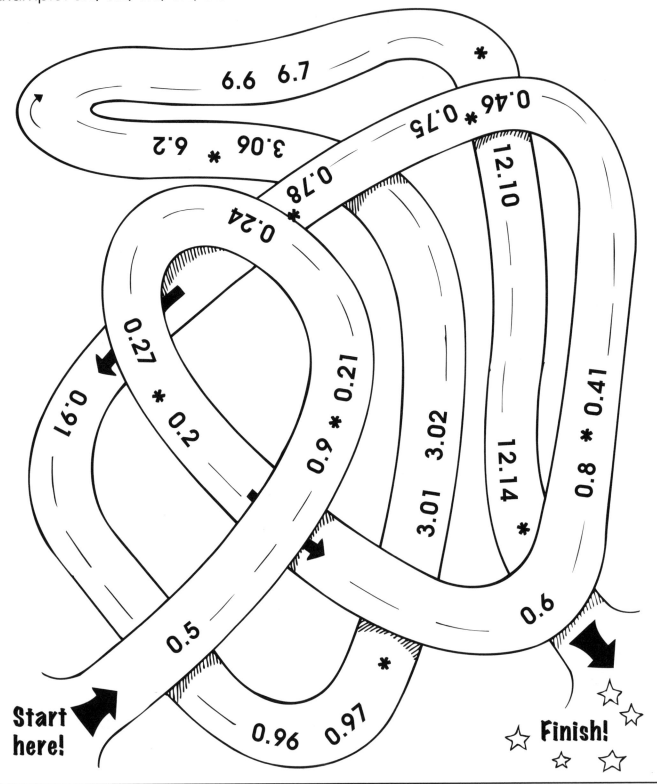

Rounding decimals

When rounding to the nearest number, if it is 5 or more, round up. If it is 4 or less, round down.

7 ↖
6.5

6.4 ↘
6

Round to the nearest whole number.

25.5 = 26
25.4 = 25

Round to the nearest tenth.

3.85 = 3.9
3.64 = 3.6

Round to the nearest whole number.

1. 3.67 _____   6.8 _____   11.4 _____   5.9 _____

2. 21.24 _____   10.51 _____   4.9 _____   14.2 _____

3. 8.6 _____   7.8 _____   9.21 _____   10.9 _____

4. 9.7 _____   10.3 _____   8.3 _____   7.4 _____

Round to the nearest tenth.

5. 6.29 _____   10.68 _____   14.83 _____   6.84 _____

6. 3.48 _____   24.37 _____   17.47 _____   28.15 _____

7. 5.49 _____   10.43 _____   3.56 _____   6.26 _____

8. 17.64 _____   112.26 _____   9.42 _____   400.67 _____

What is math good for? Who is math good for? It is good . . .
To find out, color in all decimals that round to 8 or 9 yellow. Color the rest red.

7.6	6.2	8.7	7.3	8.3	4.6	8.8	3.7	8.6
9.3	8.4	7.9	9.9	9.2	6.8	9.3	6.9	7.8
5.8	6.8	8.8	6.4	7.7	8.5	7.9	4.3	8.2

Name

Adding decimals
Unit 4

Line up the decimal
points. Write the decimal
point in the answer.

```
  3 . 4 2
+ 4 . 8 9
---------
```

Add.

```
  1   1
  3 . 4 2
+ 4 . 8 9
---------
  8 . 3 1
```

Add. Complete the cross-number puzzle.

Across:

1.
```
  17.21
+  8.42
```

3.
```
  7.64
+ 3.91
```

5.
```
  3.9
+ 0.8
```

7.
```
  7.6
+ 2.9
```

8.
```
  3.41
+ 1.89
```

9.
```
  0.61
+ 0.49
```

12.
```
  7.92
+ 0.42
```

14.
```
  1.3
+ 0.9
```

Down:

1.
```
  17.24
+  8.09
```

2.
```
  60.42
+  8.19
```

4.
```
  3.64
+ 1.95
```

5.
```
  3.04
+ 0.99
```

6.
```
  6.58
+ 0.94
```

7.
```
  0.42
+ 0.59
```

10.
```
  0.81
+ 0.92
```

11.
```
  25.14
+  2.98
```

13.
```
  $31.42
+   9.81
```

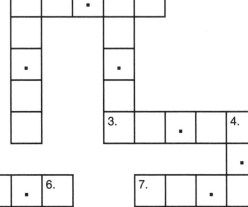

Name

Subtracting decimals

Line up the decimal points. Place a decimal point in the answer.

```
  2 3 . 4
-     8 . 5
```

Subtract.

```
  1 12 1
  2 3 . 4
-     8 . 5
  1 4 . 9
```

Subtract. Complete the cross-number puzzle.

Across:

3.
```
  14.6
-  2.9
```

4.
```
  0.6
- 0.2
```

5.
```
  6.8
- 2.9
```

7.
```
  5.6
- 2.8
```

9.
```
  30.4
-  8.2
```

11.
```
  21.42
- 18.29
```

13.
```
  5.84
- 1.38
```

14.
```
  6.5
- 0.9
```

15.
```
  3.6
- 1.9
```

16.
```
  2.8
- 1.9
```

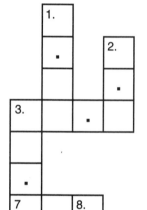

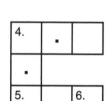

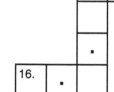

Down:

1.
```
  3.42
- 1.81
```

2.
```
  3.9
- 1.2
```

3.
```
  23.4
-  8.2
```

4.
```
  0.7
- 0.4
```

6.
```
  9.42
- 0.09
```

8.
```
  9.8
- 1.6
```

10.
```
  4.29
- 1.82
```

11.
```
  5.42
- 1.79
```

12.
```
  3.42
- 1.89
```

15.
```
  13.2
-  2.3
```

Name

Subtracting decimals with different place values   Unit 4

Add a decimal point
and zeroes where
regrouping is needed.
Place a decimal point
in the answer.

$$\begin{array}{r} 9.00 \\ -\ 7.76 \\ \hline . \end{array}$$

Regroup.

$$\begin{array}{r} {}^{8}\ {}^{9} \\ \cancel{9}.\cancel{\cancel{0}}^{1}\cancel{0}^{1}0 \\ -\ 7.76 \\ \hline . \end{array}$$

Subtract.

$$\begin{array}{r} {}^{8}\ {}^{9} \\ \cancel{9}.\cancel{\cancel{0}}^{1}\cancel{0}^{1}0 \\ -\ 7.76 \\ \hline 1.24 \end{array}$$

Subtract.

1. $\begin{array}{r} 6 \\ -\ 3.7 \\ \hline \end{array}$

2. $\begin{array}{r} 3 \\ -\ 1.8 \\ \hline \end{array}$

3. $\begin{array}{r} 2.1 \\ -\ 1.46 \\ \hline \end{array}$

4. $\begin{array}{r} 9 \\ -\ 2.8 \\ \hline \end{array}$

5. $\begin{array}{r} 4 \\ -\ 1.6 \\ \hline \end{array}$

6. $\begin{array}{r} 8 \\ -\ 2.4 \\ \hline \end{array}$

7. $\begin{array}{r} 5 \\ -\ 1.82 \\ \hline \end{array}$

8. $\begin{array}{r} 6.2 \\ -\ 3.46 \\ \hline \end{array}$

9. $\begin{array}{r} 3.5 \\ -\ 2.67 \\ \hline \end{array}$

10. $\begin{array}{r} 9.6 \\ -\ 2 \\ \hline \end{array}$

11. $\begin{array}{r} 7.3 \\ -\ 4.28 \\ \hline \end{array}$

12. $\begin{array}{r} 6 \\ -\ 2.13 \\ \hline \end{array}$

13. $\begin{array}{r} 27 \\ -\ 13.84 \\ \hline \end{array}$

14. $\begin{array}{r} 7.3 \\ -\ 2.84 \\ \hline \end{array}$

15. $\begin{array}{r} 4 \\ -\ 2.9 \\ \hline \end{array}$

16. $\begin{array}{r} 5 \\ -\ 1.64 \\ \hline \end{array}$

17. $\begin{array}{r} 8.97 \\ -\ 5.6 \\ \hline \end{array}$

18. $\begin{array}{r} 8 \\ -\ 3.64 \\ \hline \end{array}$

19. $\begin{array}{r} 12 \\ -\ 4.8 \\ \hline \end{array}$

20. $\begin{array}{r} 24.8 \\ -\ 3.94 \\ \hline \end{array}$

 The ultimate challenge! Match the decimals to produce the correct answers. Can you do all five?

A. $\begin{array}{r} 3 \\ -\ \\ \hline 2.4 \end{array}$

B. $\begin{array}{r} 3.4 \\ -\ \\ \hline 0.35 \end{array}$

C. $\begin{array}{r} 6.1 \\ -\ \\ \hline 2.56 \end{array}$

D. $\begin{array}{r} 8 \\ -\ \\ \hline 1.25 \end{array}$

E. $\begin{array}{r} 25.4 \\ -\ \\ \hline 14.28 \end{array}$

Missing decimals: 6.75   3.54   11.12   0.6   3.05

Name

Read the question. Use an extra piece of paper to write problems down and solve them. Fill in the circle beside the best answer.

 Example:

Which problem is written correctly?

3.46	7.48	16.40	
− 3.9	− 12.6	− 11.92	NG
Ⓐ	Ⓑ	Ⓒ	Ⓓ

If you are not sure what the answer is, skip it and come back to it later.

Answer: C because the decimal points are all lined up.

Now try these. You have 20 minutes. Continue until you see ⬡STOP.

1.

3.97	12.35	11.94	12.53	4.41
+ 8.38	Ⓐ	Ⓑ	Ⓒ	Ⓓ

2.

7	5.94	4.46	4.36	5.64
− 2.64	Ⓐ	Ⓑ	Ⓒ	Ⓓ

---

3. Compare the decimals using >, <, or =.

16.04 ◯ 16.40

>	<	=	NG
Ⓐ	Ⓑ	Ⓒ	Ⓓ

---

4. Identify the decimal.

Ⓐ 0.22   Ⓑ 2.4

Ⓒ 24.6   Ⓓ 2.04

GO ON ▷

Unit 4 Test

5. Round to the nearest whole number.

23.48

24 (A)   22 (B)   32 (C)   NG (D)

6. Compare using >, <, or =.

31.48 ◯ 31.29

> (A)   < (B)   = (C)   NG (D)

7.

$$\begin{array}{r} 11 \\ -\ \ 3.6 \\ \hline \end{array}$$

8.4 (A)   7.6 (B)   7.9 (C)   7.4 (D)

8.

$$\begin{array}{r} 488.24 \\ +\ \ \ 9.87 \\ \hline \end{array}$$

498.11 (A)   500.21 (B)   499.82 (C)   478.37 (D)

9. Round to the nearest tenth.

114.48

115.6 (A)   114.5 (B)   114.4 (C)   114 (D)

10. Which set of decimals is ordered from least to greatest?

(A) 0.9, 0.6, 0.4, 0.3   (B) 2.1, 8.2, 2.6, 5.8

(C) 6.1, 6.2, 6.3, 6.4   (D) NG

11. Which decimal matches this fraction?

$\dfrac{34}{100}$

0.3 (A)   0.34 (B)   3.4 (C)   34.0 (D)

GO ON

12.

```
    4
-  2.78
```

2.23 Ⓐ   2.42 Ⓑ   1.22 Ⓒ   6.78 Ⓓ

13.

```
   6.72
-  4.66
```

1.86 Ⓐ   2.43 Ⓑ   2.88 Ⓒ   2.06 Ⓓ

14.

```
   31.48
+  29.79
```

51.48 Ⓐ   61.27 Ⓑ   63.49 Ⓒ   1.69 Ⓓ

15. Compare the decimals using >, <, or =.

113.8 113.4

$>$ Ⓐ $<$ Ⓑ $=$ Ⓒ   NG Ⓓ

16. Identify the decimal.

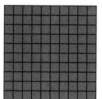 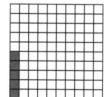

Ⓐ 4.6   Ⓑ 1.05

Ⓒ 1.5   Ⓓ 0.15

17.

```
   8.4
-  6.74
```

1.75 Ⓐ   3.24 Ⓑ   1.66 Ⓒ   NG Ⓓ

18. Order the decimals from least to greatest.

```
3.15              3.13
          3.12
    3.14
```

Ⓐ 3.12, 3.15, 3.14, 3.13

Ⓑ 3.15, 3.13, 3.12, 3.14

Ⓒ 3.12, 3.13, 3.14, 3.15

Ⓓ 3.13, 3.12, 3.14, 3.15

GO ON ▷

19.

$$16.13$$
$$-\ 0.27$$

16.80 Ⓐ

14.89 Ⓑ

15.86 Ⓒ

16.40 Ⓓ

20. How many zeroes are needed to regroup and subtract after you add a decimal point?

$$8$$
$$-\ 1.47$$

1 Ⓐ

2 Ⓑ

none Ⓒ

NG Ⓓ

Bill's Market rounds up to the nearest whole number on all produce sales. Tammy bought tomatoes for her restaurant on three different days:

Monday: 3.2 lbs.

Tuesday: 5.1 lbs.

Wednesday: 6.4 lbs.

The price was $4.00 per pound.

Why is this bad for Tammy?

Clue: 1. Round up each sale to the nearest whole number.

2. As you round up, find the total sum of extra tenths included in each sale.

3. Multiply this sum by $4.00 to see the extra amount paid.

_____

_____

_____

How much extra was she charged?

_____

_____

Midway Review Test Name Grid

Write your name in pencil in the boxes along the top. Begin with your last name. Fill in as many letters as will fit. Then follow the columns straight down and bubble in the letters that correspond with the letters in your name. Complete the rest of the information the same way. You may use a piece of scrap paper to help you keep your place.

STUDENT'S NAME

LAST											FIRST						MI
○	○	○	○	○	○	○	○	○	○	○	○	○	○	○	○	○	○
Ⓐ	Ⓐ	Ⓐ	Ⓐ	Ⓐ	Ⓐ	Ⓐ	Ⓐ	Ⓐ	Ⓐ	Ⓐ	Ⓐ	Ⓐ	Ⓐ	Ⓐ	Ⓐ	Ⓐ	Ⓐ
Ⓑ	Ⓑ	Ⓑ	Ⓑ	Ⓑ	Ⓑ	Ⓑ	Ⓑ	Ⓑ	Ⓑ	Ⓑ	Ⓑ	Ⓑ	Ⓑ	Ⓑ	Ⓑ	Ⓑ	Ⓑ
Ⓒ	Ⓒ	Ⓒ	Ⓒ	Ⓒ	Ⓒ	Ⓒ	Ⓒ	Ⓒ	Ⓒ	Ⓒ	Ⓒ	Ⓒ	Ⓒ	Ⓒ	Ⓒ	Ⓒ	Ⓒ
Ⓓ	Ⓓ	Ⓓ	Ⓓ	Ⓓ	Ⓓ	Ⓓ	Ⓓ	Ⓓ	Ⓓ	Ⓓ	Ⓓ	Ⓓ	Ⓓ	Ⓓ	Ⓓ	Ⓓ	Ⓓ
Ⓔ	Ⓔ	Ⓔ	Ⓔ	Ⓔ	Ⓔ	Ⓔ	Ⓔ	Ⓔ	Ⓔ	Ⓔ	Ⓔ	Ⓔ	Ⓔ	Ⓔ	Ⓔ	Ⓔ	Ⓔ
Ⓕ	Ⓕ	Ⓕ	Ⓕ	Ⓕ	Ⓕ	Ⓕ	Ⓕ	Ⓕ	Ⓕ	Ⓕ	Ⓕ	Ⓕ	Ⓕ	Ⓕ	Ⓕ	Ⓕ	Ⓕ
Ⓖ	Ⓖ	Ⓖ	Ⓖ	Ⓖ	Ⓖ	Ⓖ	Ⓖ	Ⓖ	Ⓖ	Ⓖ	Ⓖ	Ⓖ	Ⓖ	Ⓖ	Ⓖ	Ⓖ	Ⓖ
Ⓗ	Ⓗ	Ⓗ	Ⓗ	Ⓗ	Ⓗ	Ⓗ	Ⓗ	Ⓗ	Ⓗ	Ⓗ	Ⓗ	Ⓗ	Ⓗ	Ⓗ	Ⓗ	Ⓗ	Ⓗ
Ⓘ	Ⓘ	Ⓘ	Ⓘ	Ⓘ	Ⓘ	Ⓘ	Ⓘ	Ⓘ	Ⓘ	Ⓘ	Ⓘ	Ⓘ	Ⓘ	Ⓘ	Ⓘ	Ⓘ	Ⓘ
Ⓙ	Ⓙ	Ⓙ	Ⓙ	Ⓙ	Ⓙ	Ⓙ	Ⓙ	Ⓙ	Ⓙ	Ⓙ	Ⓙ	Ⓙ	Ⓙ	Ⓙ	Ⓙ	Ⓙ	Ⓙ
Ⓚ	Ⓚ	Ⓚ	Ⓚ	Ⓚ	Ⓚ	Ⓚ	Ⓚ	Ⓚ	Ⓚ	Ⓚ	Ⓚ	Ⓚ	Ⓚ	Ⓚ	Ⓚ	Ⓚ	Ⓚ
Ⓛ	Ⓛ	Ⓛ	Ⓛ	Ⓛ	Ⓛ	Ⓛ	Ⓛ	Ⓛ	Ⓛ	Ⓛ	Ⓛ	Ⓛ	Ⓛ	Ⓛ	Ⓛ	Ⓛ	Ⓛ
Ⓜ	Ⓜ	Ⓜ	Ⓜ	Ⓜ	Ⓜ	Ⓜ	Ⓜ	Ⓜ	Ⓜ	Ⓜ	Ⓜ	Ⓜ	Ⓜ	Ⓜ	Ⓜ	Ⓜ	Ⓜ
Ⓝ	Ⓝ	Ⓝ	Ⓝ	Ⓝ	Ⓝ	Ⓝ	Ⓝ	Ⓝ	Ⓝ	Ⓝ	Ⓝ	Ⓝ	Ⓝ	Ⓝ	Ⓝ	Ⓝ	Ⓝ
Ⓞ	Ⓞ	Ⓞ	Ⓞ	Ⓞ	Ⓞ	Ⓞ	Ⓞ	Ⓞ	Ⓞ	Ⓞ	Ⓞ	Ⓞ	Ⓞ	Ⓞ	Ⓞ	Ⓞ	Ⓞ
Ⓟ	Ⓟ	Ⓟ	Ⓟ	Ⓟ	Ⓟ	Ⓟ	Ⓟ	Ⓟ	Ⓟ	Ⓟ	Ⓟ	Ⓟ	Ⓟ	Ⓟ	Ⓟ	Ⓟ	Ⓟ
Ⓠ	Ⓠ	Ⓠ	Ⓠ	Ⓠ	Ⓠ	Ⓠ	Ⓠ	Ⓠ	Ⓠ	Ⓠ	Ⓠ	Ⓠ	Ⓠ	Ⓠ	Ⓠ	Ⓠ	Ⓠ
Ⓡ	Ⓡ	Ⓡ	Ⓡ	Ⓡ	Ⓡ	Ⓡ	Ⓡ	Ⓡ	Ⓡ	Ⓡ	Ⓡ	Ⓡ	Ⓡ	Ⓡ	Ⓡ	Ⓡ	Ⓡ
Ⓢ	Ⓢ	Ⓢ	Ⓢ	Ⓢ	Ⓢ	Ⓢ	Ⓢ	Ⓢ	Ⓢ	Ⓢ	Ⓢ	Ⓢ	Ⓢ	Ⓢ	Ⓢ	Ⓢ	Ⓢ
Ⓣ	Ⓣ	Ⓣ	Ⓣ	Ⓣ	Ⓣ	Ⓣ	Ⓣ	Ⓣ	Ⓣ	Ⓣ	Ⓣ	Ⓣ	Ⓣ	Ⓣ	Ⓣ	Ⓣ	Ⓣ
Ⓤ	Ⓤ	Ⓤ	Ⓤ	Ⓤ	Ⓤ	Ⓤ	Ⓤ	Ⓤ	Ⓤ	Ⓤ	Ⓤ	Ⓤ	Ⓤ	Ⓤ	Ⓤ	Ⓤ	Ⓤ
Ⓥ	Ⓥ	Ⓥ	Ⓥ	Ⓥ	Ⓥ	Ⓥ	Ⓥ	Ⓥ	Ⓥ	Ⓥ	Ⓥ	Ⓥ	Ⓥ	Ⓥ	Ⓥ	Ⓥ	Ⓥ
Ⓦ	Ⓦ	Ⓦ	Ⓦ	Ⓦ	Ⓦ	Ⓦ	Ⓦ	Ⓦ	Ⓦ	Ⓦ	Ⓦ	Ⓦ	Ⓦ	Ⓦ	Ⓦ	Ⓦ	Ⓦ
Ⓧ	Ⓧ	Ⓧ	Ⓧ	Ⓧ	Ⓧ	Ⓧ	Ⓧ	Ⓧ	Ⓧ	Ⓧ	Ⓧ	Ⓧ	Ⓧ	Ⓧ	Ⓧ	Ⓧ	Ⓧ
Ⓨ	Ⓨ	Ⓨ	Ⓨ	Ⓨ	Ⓨ	Ⓨ	Ⓨ	Ⓨ	Ⓨ	Ⓨ	Ⓨ	Ⓨ	Ⓨ	Ⓨ	Ⓨ	Ⓨ	Ⓨ
Ⓩ	Ⓩ	Ⓩ	Ⓩ	Ⓩ	Ⓩ	Ⓩ	Ⓩ	Ⓩ	Ⓩ	Ⓩ	Ⓩ	Ⓩ	Ⓩ	Ⓩ	Ⓩ	Ⓩ	Ⓩ

SCHOOL

TEACHER

FEMALE ○ MALE ○

DATE OF BIRTH

MONTH	DAY	YEAR
JAN ○	⓪ ⓪	⓪ ⓪
FEB ○	① ①	① ①
MAR ○	② ②	② ②
APR ○	③ ③	③ ③
MAY ○	④	④ ④
JUN ○	⑤	⑤ ⑤
JUL ○	⑥	⑥ ⑥
AUG ○	⑦	⑦ ⑦
SEP ○	⑧	⑧ ⑧
OCT ○	⑨	⑨ ⑨
NOV ○		
DEC ○		

GRADE ③ ④ ⑤

Midway Review Test Answer Sheet

Pay close attention when transferring your answers. Fill in the bubbles neatly and completely. You may use a piece of scrap paper to help you keep your place.

SAMPLES
A Ⓐ Ⓑ ● Ⓓ
B Ⓕ ● Ⓗ Ⓙ

1 Ⓐ Ⓑ Ⓒ Ⓓ
2 Ⓕ Ⓖ Ⓗ Ⓙ
3 Ⓐ Ⓑ Ⓒ Ⓓ
4 Ⓕ Ⓖ Ⓗ Ⓙ
5 Ⓐ Ⓑ Ⓒ Ⓓ
6 Ⓕ Ⓖ Ⓗ Ⓙ
7 Ⓐ Ⓑ Ⓒ Ⓓ
8 Ⓕ Ⓖ Ⓗ Ⓙ
9 Ⓐ Ⓑ Ⓒ Ⓓ
10 Ⓕ Ⓖ Ⓗ Ⓙ
11 Ⓐ Ⓑ Ⓒ Ⓓ
12 Ⓕ Ⓖ Ⓗ Ⓙ
13 Ⓐ Ⓑ Ⓒ Ⓓ
14 Ⓕ Ⓖ Ⓗ Ⓙ
15 Ⓐ Ⓑ Ⓒ Ⓓ
16 Ⓕ Ⓖ Ⓗ Ⓙ
17 Ⓐ Ⓑ Ⓒ Ⓓ
18 Ⓕ Ⓖ Ⓗ Ⓙ
19 Ⓐ Ⓑ Ⓒ Ⓓ
20 Ⓕ Ⓖ Ⓗ Ⓙ
21 Ⓐ Ⓑ Ⓒ Ⓓ
22 Ⓕ Ⓖ Ⓗ Ⓙ
23 Ⓐ Ⓑ Ⓒ Ⓓ
24 Ⓕ Ⓖ Ⓗ Ⓙ
25 Ⓐ Ⓑ Ⓒ Ⓓ

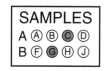

Midway Review Test

Read the question. Use an extra piece of paper to work on problems and keep your place on the score sheet. Fill in the circle beside the best answer.

☐ Example:

Solve. Remember to do the operation inside parentheses first.

$(8 + 9) - 4 = \boxed{}$

(A) 21   (B) 13

(C) 17   (D) NG

Answer: B because 17 – 4 = 13

Now try these. You have 25 minutes.

Continue until you see STOP.

Remember your Helping Hand Strategies:

 1. Sometimes the correct answer is not given. Fill in the circle beside NG if no answer is correct.

 2. Always read each question carefully.

 3. Always read the question twice. Does your answer make sense?

 4. If you are not sure what the answer is, skip it and come back to it later.

---

1. Round 384,211 to the nearest hundred thousand.

300,000   800,000   400,000   380,000
(A)   (B)   (C)   (D)

---

2. Compare using >, <, or =.

5,284 ◯ 4,842

>   <   =   NG
(F)   (G)   (H)   (J)

3.

    42
  528
+ 161

661   735   842   731
(A)   (B)   (C)   (D)

GO ON ▷

Midway Review Test

4.

$$\begin{array}{r} 3,842 \\ -\ 1,396 \end{array}$$

3,149 **(F)** 2,446 **(G)** 2,548 **(H)** 5,238 **(J)**

5. $(16 - 9) + 3 = \square$

16 **(A)** 14 **(B)** 11 **(C)** 10 **(D)**

6. $5 + (11 - 6) = \square$

10 **(F)** 6 **(G)** 14 **(H)** 1 **(J)**

7.

$$\begin{array}{r} 8,000 \\ -\ 4,623 \end{array}$$

4,654 **(A)** 2,198 **(B)** 3,377 **(C)** NG **(D)**

8. What is the correct regrouping for this problem?

$$\begin{array}{r} 1,465 \\ \times\ \ \ 7 \end{array}$$

1
1465 **(F)**

343
1465 **(G)**

142
1465 **(H)**

NG **(J)**

9.

$$\begin{array}{r} 49 \\ \times\ \ 6 \end{array}$$

742 **(A)** 298 **(B)** 345 **(C)** 294 **(D)**

10.

$$\begin{array}{r} 398 \\ \times\ \ 4 \end{array}$$

2,480 **(F)** 1,592 **(G)** 3,980 **(H)** 1,262 **(J)**

GO ON

Midway Review Test

11.
$$\begin{array}{r} 48 \\ \times\ 16 \\ \hline \end{array}$$

480 (A)   674 (B)   768 (C)   336 (D)

12.
$$\begin{array}{r} 238 \\ \times\ 36 \\ \hline \end{array}$$

9,429 (F)   8,568 (G)   7,429 (H)   2,142 (J)

13. Estimate the product.

$$\begin{array}{r} \$9.21 \\ \times\ 8 \\ \hline \end{array}$$

$72.00 (A) $90.00 (B) $86.00 (C)   NG (D)

14.

$$6\overline{)45}$$

9 R2 (F)   7 R3 (G)   6 R5 (H)   8 R1 (J)

15. The remainder can be any amount, as long as it is less than the _____.

quotient
divisor
$$2\overline{)683}\ ^{341}$$
dividend

(A) quotient (the answer)

(B) dividend (number inside the division bar)

(C) divisor (number outside the division bar)

(D) NG

GO ON

Midway Review Test

16.

$3\overline{)170}$

56 R2 (F) 74 R1 (G) 69 R4 (H) NG (J)

17.

$6\overline{)748}$

342 R1 (A) 549 R2 (B) 124 R4 (C) 151 R5 (D)

18.

$4\overline{)827}$

206 R3 (F) 304 R2 (G) 180 R3 (H) 304 R2 (J)

19.

$2\overline{)\$9.26}$

$2.99 (A) $4.63 (B) $5.81 (C) $3.26 (D)

20. Compare using >, <, or =.

0.65 ◯ 0.51

\> (F) < (G) = (H) NG (J)

21.

$$\begin{array}{r} 14.84 \\ +\quad 8.95 \\ \hline \end{array}$$

23.45 (A) 25.48 (B) 22.92 (C) NG (D)

22. Order the decimals from least to greatest.

0.75	0.73
0.72	0.74

(F) 0.73, 0.75, 0.72, 0.74

(G) 0.72, 0.73, 0.74, 0.75

(H) 0.75, 0.72, 0.73, 0.74

(J) 0.72, 0.74, 0.75, 0.73

GO ON ⇒

Midway Review Test

23.

4.7
− 3.9

1.2
Ⓐ

0.8
Ⓑ

2.6
Ⓒ

8.6
Ⓓ

24.

6
− 1.49

4.51
Ⓕ

5.49
Ⓖ

6.04
Ⓗ

7.49
Ⓙ

25. Round to the nearest whole number.

4.86

7
Ⓐ

8
Ⓑ

5
Ⓒ

NG
Ⓓ

Is rounding of numbers helpful in life? When is it helpful for you or your family?

_____

_____

_____

_____

_____

Name

Line segments, lines, and rays

The straight path between points X and Y is a **line segment**. (segment XY)

A **line** is a straight path that goes unending in two directions. (line CD)

A **ray** is a straight path that begins at a point and goes unending in one direction. (ray TX)

Lines that never meet are called **parallel lines**.

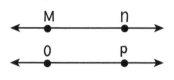

Lines that cross are called **intersecting lines**.

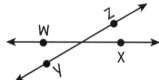

Lines that cross at right angles are called **perpendicular lines**.

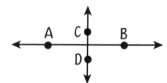

Using the appropriate letters, identify each as a **line segment**, **line**, or **ray**.

1. _____

2. _____

3. _____

4. _____

5. _____

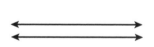

6. _____

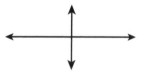

7. _____

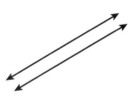

8. _____

Identify as **parallel lines**, **intersecting lines**, or **perpendicular lines**.

9. _____   10. _____   11. _____   12. _____

Draw two parallel lines. Draw two intersecting lines across the two parallel lines.

Angles

The point at which two rays meet to form an angle is called a **vertex**. Point n is the vertex.

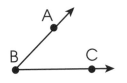

An angle that is less than 90° is called an **acute** angle.

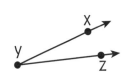

An angle that is 90° is a **right** angle. A square is made up of right angles.

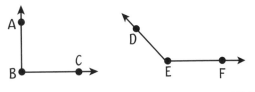

An angle greater than 90° is called an **obtuse** angle.

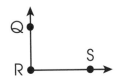

Identify each angle below as either **acute**, **right**, or **obtuse**.

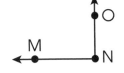

1. _____

2. _____

3. _____

4. _____

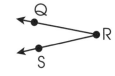

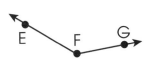

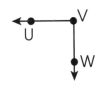

5. _____

6. _____

7. _____

8. _____

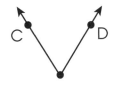

9. _____

10. _____

Name

Points on a grid

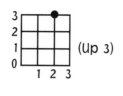

Here it is!

(2, 3)

The ordered pair tells where the point is on this grid. (Over and up!)

The first number tells how many units the point is to the right of the zero. (Over 2)

The second numbers tells how many units to go up. (Up 3)

(2, 3) (Over 2)   (Up 3)

Write the ordered pair.

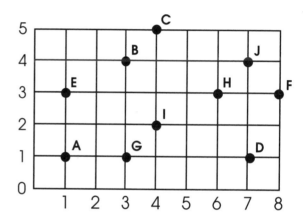

1. A = (____ , ____)   2. F = (____ , ____)

3. B = (____ , ____)   4. G = (____ , ____)

5. C = (____ , ____)   6. H = (____ , ____)

7. D = (____ , ____)   8. I = (____ , ____)

9. E = (____ , ____)   10. J = (____ , ____)

What is the secret message? Write the letters for each ordered pair.

1. (4, 6) _____   4. (1, 1) _____   7. (6, 2) _____   16. (5, 1) _____

2. (7, 7) _____   5. (1, 1) _____   8. (4, 3) _____   17. (1, 1) _____

3. (5, 1) _____   6. (1, 4) _____   9. (0, 5) _____   18. (1, 4) _____

10. (8, 3) _____   19. (4, 3) _____

11. (2, 7) _____   20. (2, 7) _____

12. (6, 5) _____   21. (2, 4) _____

13. (3, 2) _____   22. (8, 1) _____

14. (1, 4) _____   23. (5, 1) _____

15. (5, 1) _____   24. (7, 4) _____

_____

Name

Similar and congruent figures

Figures that are the same shape but not the same size are called **similar**.

Figures that are the same size and shape are called **congruent**.

Using a ruler, connect the dots to draw lines to the figures that are similar. Are the two figures you made by connecting the lines similar? _____

 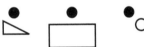

Using a ruler, connect the dots to draw lines to the figures that are congruent. Are the two figures you made by connecting the lines congruent? _____

Name

Polygons   Unit 5

When three or more line segments come together, they form a **polygon**. The points where the line segments meet are called vertices.

A polygon with 3 sides: triangle

A polygon with 4 sides: quadrilateral

A polygon with 5 sides: pentagon

Identify each type of polygon as a **triangle**, **quadrilateral**, or **pentagon**.

1. _____

2. _____

3. _____

4. _____

5. _____

6. _____

7. _____

8. _____

9. _____

10. _____

11. _____

12. _____

A **parallelogram** is a special type of quadrilateral that has opposite sides that are parallel and the same length.   parallel

A **rectangle** is a parallelogram that has four right angles.

A **square** is a rectangle with four sides equal in length.

Identify each type of polygon as a **parallelogram**, **rectangle**, or **square**.

13. _____

14. _____

15. _____

16. _____

Name

Perimeter and area

The **perimeter** is the distance around an object.

Add the sides together to find the perimeter.

8 cm + 2 cm + 8 cm + 2 cm = 20 centimeters

The **area** is the amount of square units within that object.

Multiply the two sides of the object to find the area.

2 cm x 8 cm = 16 square centimeters

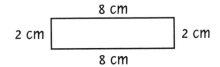

Find the perimeters of these polygons.

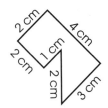

1. P = _____ cm

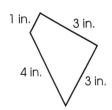

2. P = _____ in.

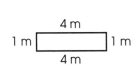

3. P = _____ m

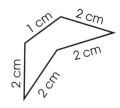

4. P = _____ cm

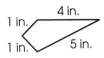

5. P = _____ in.

6. P = _____ yd.

7. P = _____ ft.

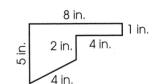

8. P = _____ in.

Find the areas of these polygons.

9. A = _____ sq. cm

10. A = _____ sq. yd.

11. A = _____ sq. ft.

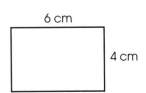

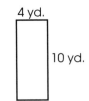

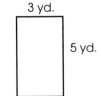

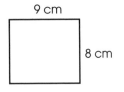

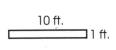

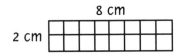

12. A = _____ sq. m

13. A = _____ sq. yd.

14. A = _____ sq. cm

Volume

You can find the **volume** by counting the cubic units that a figure contains. The volume is written in cubic units.

4 cm x 2 cm x 2 cm = 16 cubic centimeters

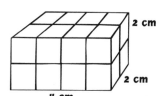

You can also multiply the length, by the width, by the height (l x w x h = v).

2 cm x 4 cm x 6 cm = 48 cubic centimeters

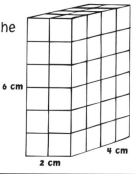

Find the volume.

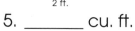

1. _____ cu. cm   2. _____ cu. yd.   3. _____ cu. in.   4. _____ cu. m

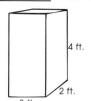
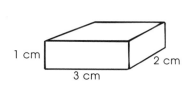
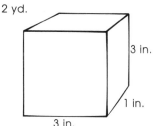

5. _____ cu. ft.   6. _____ cu. cm   7. _____ cu. ft.   8. _____ cu. m

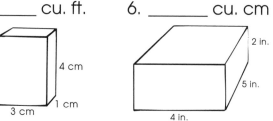
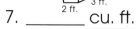
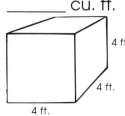
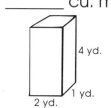

9. _____ cu. cm   10. _____ cu. in.   11. _____ cu. ft.   12. _____ cu. yd.

What is the total volume of this model of a skyscraper?

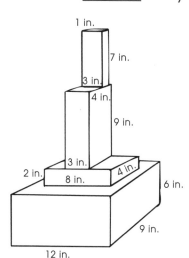

level four volume = _____

level three volume = _____

level two volume = _____

level one volume = _____

_____ cubic inches

Cubes, rectangular prisms, spheres, pyramids, cylinders, and cones

Unit 5

Solid figures can have many vertices, edges, and faces.

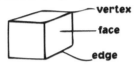

- vertex
- face
- edge

Or, they can have none at all!

cubes (6 faces)

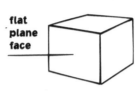

flat plane face

rectangular prisms (6 faces)

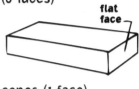

flat face

pyramids (4 or more faces)

flat face

spheres (no faces)

cylinders (2 faces)

flat face

cones (1 face)

flat face

Identify the solid figures.

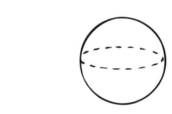 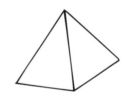 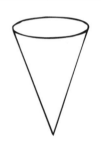

1. _____

2. _____

3. _____

4. _____

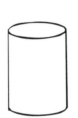   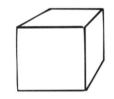

5. _____

6. _____

7. _____

8. _____

9. _____

10. _____

11. _____

12. _____

13. _____

14. _____

15. _____

16. _____

Symmetry

If you can fold a figure in half, and both sides are identical, it is said to be **symmetrical**.

A line of symmetry will divide a figure in half. Each side will be identical in shape.

Some figures have many different lines of symmetry.

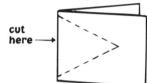

cut here →

Is each figure symmetrical? Write **yes** or **no**.

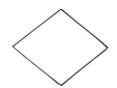

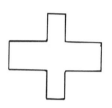

1. _____ 2. _____ 3. _____ 4. _____ 5. _____

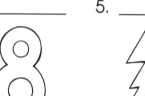

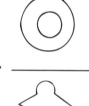

6. _____ 7. _____ 8. _____ 9. _____ 10. _____

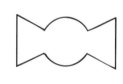

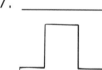

11. _____ 12. _____ 13. _____ 14. _____ 15. _____

Draw a line of symmetry through each figure.

16. 17. 18. 19. 20.

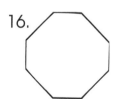

21. 22. 23. 24. 25.

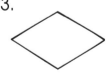

Name

Read the question. Use an extra piece of paper to write problems down and solve them. Fill in the circle beside the best answer.

☐ Example:

Are these two figures similar or congruent?

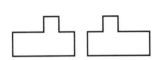

(A) similar

(B) congruent

(C) NG

Cross out answers you know are wrong.

Answer: B because the figures are the same size and shape.

Now try these. You have 20 minutes. Continue until you see ⬡STOP.

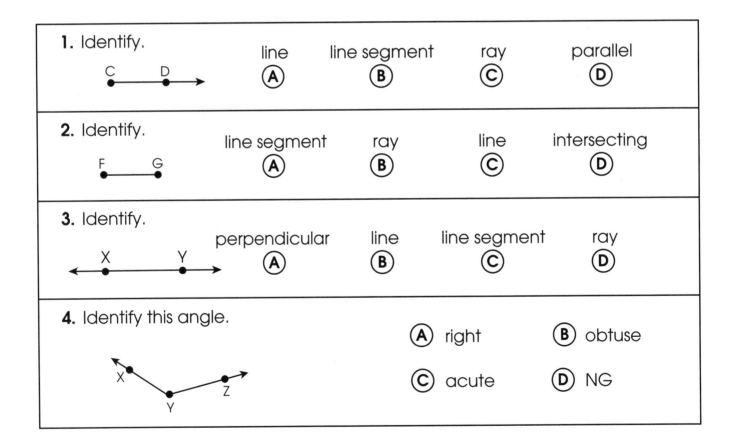

1. Identify.

C   D

line	line segment	ray	parallel
(A)	(B)	(C)	(D)

2. Identify.

F   G

line segment	ray	line	intersecting
(A)	(B)	(C)	(D)

3. Identify.

X   Y

perpendicular	line	line segment	ray
(A)	(B)	(C)	(D)

4. Identify this angle.

X   Y   Z

(A) right   (B) obtuse

(C) acute   (D) NG

GO ON ⟳

5. What is the point "B" on angle ABC called?

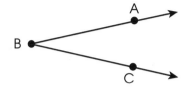

(A) ray   (B) vertex

(C) line segment   (D) NG

6. Compare these two figures.

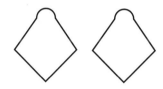

(A) similar   (B) congruent

(C) sphere   (D) NG

7. Identify this polygon.

(A) parallelogram   (B) triangle

(C) quadrilateral   (D) pentagon

8. What is the perimeter of this polygon?

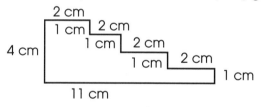

(A) 12 cm   (B) 27 cm

(C) 30 cm   (D) 25 cm

9. What type of angle is this?

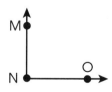

(A) acute   (B) right

(C) obtuse   (D) ray

10. Identify this polygon.

(A) quadrilateral   (B) triangle

(C) pentagon   (D) parallelogram

GO ON

11. What letter on the grid does the number pair (4, 5) represent?

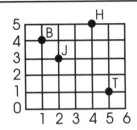

(A) J (B) T

(C) H (D) B

12. What is the area of this polygon?

10 in.

4 in.

(A) 14 sq. in. (B) 40 sq. in.

(C) 28 sq. in. (D) 22 sq. in.

13. How many lines of symmetry does this figure have?

(A) 1 (B) 2

(C) 3 (D) 0

14. Which figure is similar to the one given?

(A)

(B)

(C)

NG
(D)

15. Describe these two lines.

(A) perpendicular (B) ray

(C) parallel (D) intersecting

16. What letter on the grid does the number pair (5, 1) represent?

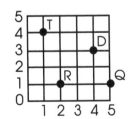

(A) Q (B) D

(C) T (D) R

GO ON

Name

17. What is the correct line of symmetry for this figure?

  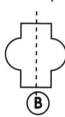

Ⓐ Ⓑ Ⓒ

NG
Ⓓ

18. Identify this figure.

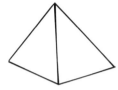

Ⓐ cone   Ⓑ sphere

Ⓒ pyramid Ⓓ cube

19. Find the volume.

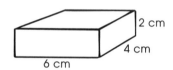

2 cm
4 cm
6 cm

Ⓐ 12 cubic centimeters

Ⓑ 47 cubic centimeters

Ⓒ 50 cubic centimeters

Ⓓ 48 cubic centimeters

20. Find the volume.

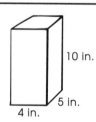

10 in.
5 in.
4 in.

Ⓐ 200 cubic inches   Ⓑ 19 cubic inches

Ⓒ 90 cubic inches   Ⓓ NG

Create a figure with
a perimeter of 20 cm.
Why is your figure correct?

_____

_____

_____

Name

Fractions of a whole

 $\frac{4}{8}$ numerator / denominator

How many parts are shaded?
4 (numerator)

How many parts is this rectangle
cut into? 8 (denominator)

Fractions of a set

 $\frac{6}{12}$

How many shapes are shaded?
6 (numerator)

How many shapes are there in all?
12 (denominator)

What is the fraction of the shaded part?

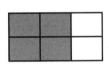

1. _____

2. _____

3. _____

4. _____

5. _____

6. _____

7. _____

8. _____

9. _____

10. _____

What fraction of the set is shaded?

11. _____

12. _____

13. _____

14. _____

15. _____

16. _____

17. _____

18. _____

19. _____

20. _____

Name

Finding fractions of whole numbers

$\frac{1}{4}$ of 16

Divide the whole number by the denominator. $16 \div 4 = 4$

Multiply this quotient by the numerator. $1 \times 4 = 4$

$\frac{1}{4}$ of 12

$12 \div 4 = 3$

$1 \times 3 = 3$

The denominator tells us how many equal groups to make. The numerator tells us how many of these groups to add together.

Find each number.

1. $\frac{1}{3}$ of 15

2. $\frac{1}{6}$ of 12

3. $\frac{1}{2}$ of 10

4. $\frac{1}{4}$ of 20

5. $\frac{1}{7}$ of 14

6. $\frac{1}{8}$ of 24

7. $\frac{1}{7}$ of 28

8. $\frac{1}{3}$ of 27

9. $\frac{1}{5}$ of 30

10. $\frac{1}{8}$ of 40

11. $\frac{1}{4}$ of 36

12. $\frac{2}{5}$ of 10

13. $\frac{1}{5}$ of 45

14. $\frac{2}{3}$ of 21

15. $\frac{4}{6}$ of 12

16. $\frac{1}{10}$ of 20

17. $\frac{1}{4}$ of 16

18. $\frac{3}{5}$ of 15

19. $\frac{1}{8}$ of 64

20. $\frac{3}{4}$ of 20

Name

Equivalent fractions

$$\frac{1}{2} = \frac{2}{4}$$

Fractions that equal the same amount are called **equivalent fractions**.

$$\frac{1}{4} = \frac{2}{8}$$

It's the same amount of pizza, the pieces are just different sizes!

Write the equivalent fractions.

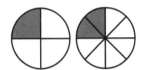

1. _____ = _____   2. _____ = _____   3. _____ = _____

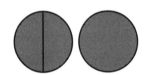

4. _____ = _____   5. _____ = _____   6. _____ = _____

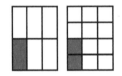

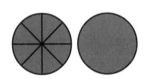

7. _____ = _____   8. _____ = _____   9. _____ = _____

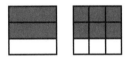

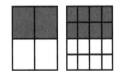

10. _____ = _____   11. _____ = _____   12. _____ = _____

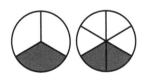

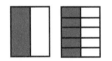

13. _____ = _____   14. _____ = _____   15. _____ = _____

         Teach & Test Math: Grade 4

Name

Reducing fractions to lowest terms

$\frac{6}{12}$

$\frac{6 \div 6}{12 \div 6} = \frac{1}{2}$

$\frac{1}{2}$

What is the greatest common factor (GCF) we can divide into both the numerator and denominator?

6 is the GCF. Divide.

Is there a common factor greater than 1 that will divide into both of these numbers? No. The fraction is reduced to lowest terms.

If the numerator and denominator are the same, it reduces to 1. More examples:

$\frac{3}{9} = \frac{3 \div 3}{9 \div 3} = \frac{1}{3}$ $\frac{4}{12} = \frac{4 \div 4}{12 \div 4} = \frac{1}{3}$ $\frac{8}{12} = \frac{8 \div 4}{12 \div 4} = \frac{2}{3}$

Reduce to lowest terms.

1. $\frac{10}{12} =$ 2. $\frac{4}{16} =$ 3. $\frac{6}{18} =$

4. $\frac{10}{15} =$ 5. $\frac{14}{16} =$ 6. $\frac{7}{21} =$

7. $\frac{5}{15} =$ 8. $\frac{4}{10} =$ 9. $\frac{9}{18} =$ 10. $\frac{8}{24} =$ 11. $\frac{4}{8} =$

12. $\frac{10}{16} =$ 13. $\frac{7}{14} =$ 14. $\frac{6}{12} =$ 15. $\frac{12}{14} =$ 16. $\frac{8}{10} =$

17. $\frac{5}{20} =$ 18. $\frac{3}{9} =$ 19. $\frac{6}{24} =$ 20. $\frac{5}{25} =$ 21. $\frac{10}{40} =$

Mixed numbers   Unit 6

If the numerator is greater than the denominator, this type of fraction is called an **improper fraction**.

An improper fraction can be written as a mixed number. Divide the numerator by the denominator. The whole number tells how many whole parts we have.

The remainder becomes the numerator, and the divisor becomes the denominator.

$$\frac{11}{5}$$

$$5 \overline{)11} \\ \begin{array}{r} 2 \\ -10 \\ \hline 1 \end{array}$$

$$5 \overline{)11} \\ \begin{array}{r} 2 \\ -10 \\ \hline 1 \end{array} = 2\frac{1}{5}$$

More examples:

$$\frac{7}{3} = \begin{array}{r} 2 \\ 3 \overline{)7} \\ -6 \\ \hline 1 \end{array} = 2\frac{1}{3}$$

$$\frac{14}{4} = \begin{array}{r} 3 \\ 4 \overline{)14} \\ -12 \\ \hline 2 \end{array} = 3\frac{2}{4} = 3\frac{1}{2}$$

Convert to mixed numbers in lowest terms.

1. $\frac{15}{7} =$ 2. $\frac{14}{4} =$ 3. $\frac{7}{3} =$ 4. $\frac{11}{5} =$ 5. $\frac{17}{9} =$

6. $\frac{13}{4} =$ 7. $\frac{16}{5} =$ 8. $\frac{11}{2} =$ 9. $\frac{10}{4} =$ 10. $\frac{21}{5} =$

11. $\frac{23}{6} =$ 12. $\frac{19}{6} =$ 13. $\frac{9}{2} =$ 14. $\frac{15}{6} =$ 15. $\frac{26}{6} =$

16. $\frac{18}{8} =$ 17. $\frac{9}{7} =$ 18. $\frac{30}{4} =$

19. $\frac{14}{5} =$ 20. $\frac{13}{8} =$ 21. $\frac{13}{6} =$

Name

Addition of fractions with like denominators   Unit 6

Question: Are the denominators the same? Yes

$$\begin{array}{r} \dfrac{4}{9} \\[2mm] +\ \dfrac{2}{9} \\ \hline \end{array}$$

Simply add the numerators. Keep the same denominator.

$$\begin{array}{r} \dfrac{4}{9} \\[2mm] +\ \dfrac{2}{9} \\ \hline \dfrac{6}{9} \end{array}$$

Reduce to lowest terms.

$$\dfrac{6 \div 3}{9 \div 3} = \dfrac{2}{3}$$

Add. Reduce to lowest terms. Change improper fractions to mixed numbers.

1. $\dfrac{2}{7}$
    $+\ \dfrac{3}{7}$

2. $\dfrac{3}{9}$
    $+\ \dfrac{4}{9}$

3. $\dfrac{2}{14}$
    $+\ \dfrac{7}{14}$

4. $\dfrac{3}{10}$
    $+\ \dfrac{3}{10}$

5. $\dfrac{4}{11}$
    $+\ \dfrac{5}{11}$

6. $\dfrac{2}{8}$
    $+\ \dfrac{4}{8}$

7. $\dfrac{3}{5}$
    $+\ \dfrac{4}{5}$

8. $\dfrac{2}{9}$
    $+\ \dfrac{5}{9}$

9. $\dfrac{3}{8}$
    $+\ \dfrac{9}{8}$

10. $\dfrac{5}{13}$
    $+\ \dfrac{5}{13}$

11. $\dfrac{4}{8}$
    $+\ \dfrac{3}{8}$

12. $\dfrac{3}{5}$
    $+\ \dfrac{1}{5}$

13. $\dfrac{4}{10}$
    $+\ \dfrac{7}{10}$

14. $\dfrac{3}{11}$
    $+\ \dfrac{4}{11}$

15. $\dfrac{4}{9}$
    $+\ \dfrac{4}{9}$

16. $\dfrac{3}{8}$
    $+\ \dfrac{7}{8}$

17. $\dfrac{5}{10}$
    $+\ \dfrac{4}{10}$

18. $\dfrac{3}{6}$
    $+\ \dfrac{2}{6}$

Name

Subtraction of fractions with like denominators

Question: Are the denominators the same? Yes

$$\frac{5}{6}$$
$$-\frac{1}{6}$$

Simply subtract the numerators. Keep the same denominator.

$$\frac{5}{6}$$
$$-\frac{1}{6}$$
$$\frac{4}{6}$$

Reduce to lowest terms.

$$\frac{4 \div 2}{6 \div 2} = \frac{2}{3}$$

Subtract. Reduce to lowest terms.

1. $\frac{3}{8}$
   $-\frac{1}{8}$

2. $\frac{5}{7}$
   $-\frac{3}{7}$

3. $\frac{4}{10}$
   $-\frac{3}{10}$

4. $\frac{7}{11}$
   $-\frac{4}{11}$

5. $\frac{6}{12}$
   $-\frac{2}{12}$

6. $\frac{6}{8}$
   $-\frac{4}{8}$

7. $\frac{11}{13}$
   $-\frac{9}{13}$

8. $\frac{7}{9}$
   $-\frac{5}{9}$

9. $\frac{7}{15}$
   $-\frac{4}{15}$

10. $\frac{5}{9}$
    $-\frac{3}{9}$

11. $\frac{5}{6}$
    $-\frac{4}{6}$

12. $\frac{4}{7}$
    $-\frac{2}{7}$

13. $\frac{7}{10}$
    $-\frac{3}{10}$

14. $\frac{9}{12}$
    $-\frac{1}{12}$

15. $\frac{13}{14}$
    $-\frac{8}{14}$

16. $\frac{9}{11}$
    $-\frac{4}{11}$

17. $\frac{15}{17}$
    $-\frac{8}{17}$

18. $\frac{10}{13}$
    $-\frac{5}{13}$

Name _____

In order to compare, you must find equivalent fractions.

$$\frac{1}{4} \bigcirc \frac{1}{8}$$

First, we must find a common denominator. Does something multiplied by 4 equal 8? Yes, 2. 8 is our common denominator.

$$\frac{1 \times 2}{4 \times 2} = \frac{2}{8}$$

Multiply the numerator and denominator by 2 to create equivalent fractions.

 $\frac{1}{4} = \frac{2}{8}$

Compare.

$$\frac{1}{4} > \frac{1}{8}$$

Compare using **>**, **<**, or **=**.

1. $\dfrac{5}{10} \bigcirc \dfrac{2}{10}$

2. $\dfrac{1}{3} \bigcirc \dfrac{2}{3}$

3. $\dfrac{5}{8} \bigcirc \dfrac{6}{8}$

4. $\dfrac{3}{10} \bigcirc \dfrac{8}{10}$

5. $\dfrac{1}{4} \bigcirc \dfrac{3}{4}$

6. $\dfrac{6}{7} \bigcirc \dfrac{3}{7}$

7. $\dfrac{4}{6} \bigcirc \dfrac{1}{6}$

8. $\dfrac{5}{9} \bigcirc \dfrac{4}{9}$

9. $\dfrac{6}{11} \bigcirc \dfrac{9}{11}$

10. $\dfrac{1}{5} \bigcirc \dfrac{3}{5}$

11. $\dfrac{3}{4} \bigcirc \dfrac{2}{4}$

12. $\dfrac{2}{3} \bigcirc \dfrac{1}{3}$

13. $\dfrac{1}{2} \bigcirc \dfrac{3}{4}$

14. $\dfrac{1}{6} \bigcirc \dfrac{2}{3}$

15. $\dfrac{3}{4} \bigcirc \dfrac{1}{8}$

16. $\dfrac{2}{4} \bigcirc \dfrac{1}{2}$

17. $\dfrac{6}{8} \bigcirc \dfrac{2}{4}$

18. $\dfrac{1}{3} \bigcirc \dfrac{2}{9}$

19. $\dfrac{4}{6} \bigcirc \dfrac{2}{3}$

20. $\dfrac{1}{5} \bigcirc \dfrac{2}{15}$

21. $\dfrac{3}{4} \bigcirc \dfrac{5}{8}$

Addition of fractions with unlike denominators

Unit 6

Create equivalent fractions with a common denominator.

$$\frac{1}{8} \qquad \frac{1 \times 2}{8 \times 2} \qquad \frac{2}{16}$$

$$+ \frac{2}{16} \qquad + \frac{2}{16} \qquad + \frac{2}{16}$$

Add.

$$\frac{2}{16}$$
$$+ \frac{2}{16}$$
$$\overline{\quad\frac{4}{16}\quad}$$

Reduce to lowest terms.

$$\frac{4 \div 4}{16 \div 4} = \frac{1}{4}$$

Add. Reduce to lowest terms.

1. $\frac{1}{5}$
   $+ \frac{1}{10}$

2. $\frac{1}{12}$
   $+ \frac{4}{6}$

3. $\frac{1}{7}$
   $+ \frac{7}{14}$

4. $\frac{3}{5}$
   $+ \frac{2}{15}$

5. $\frac{1}{2}$
   $+ \frac{1}{4}$

6. $\frac{3}{6}$
   $+ \frac{1}{3}$

7. $\frac{1}{4}$
   $+ \frac{5}{8}$

8. $\frac{1}{8}$
   $+ \frac{1}{2}$

9. $\frac{3}{7}$
   $+ \frac{3}{14}$

10. $\frac{1}{3}$
   $+ \frac{1}{6}$

11. $\frac{3}{10}$
   $+ \frac{2}{5}$

12. $\frac{1}{6}$
   $+ \frac{5}{12}$

13. $\frac{5}{10}$
   $+ \frac{2}{5}$

14. $\frac{3}{12}$
   $+ \frac{1}{4}$

15. $\frac{1}{3}$
   $+ \frac{4}{9}$

16. $\frac{1}{12}$
   $+ \frac{1}{6}$

17. $\frac{3}{10}$
   $+ \frac{1}{2}$

18. $\frac{2}{16}$
   $+ \frac{3}{8}$

19. $\frac{6}{9}$
   $+ \frac{1}{3}$

20. $\frac{1}{2}$
   $+ \frac{3}{8}$

Subtraction of fractions with unlike denominators

Unit 6

Create equivalent fractions with a common denominator.

$$\frac{8}{10} \qquad \frac{8}{10} \qquad \frac{8}{10}$$
$$-\frac{2}{5} \qquad -\frac{2 \times 2}{5 \times 2} \qquad -\frac{4}{10}$$

Subtract.

$$\frac{8}{10}$$
$$-\frac{4}{10}$$
$$\frac{4}{10}$$

Reduce to lowest terms.

$$\frac{4 \div 2}{10 \div 2} = \frac{2}{5}$$

Subtract. Reduce to lowest terms.

1. $\dfrac{3}{4}$ $-\dfrac{1}{2}$

2. $\dfrac{14}{16}$ $-\dfrac{5}{8}$

3. $\dfrac{4}{5}$ $-\dfrac{5}{10}$

COMMON DENOMINATOR

4. $\dfrac{9}{14}$ $-\dfrac{3}{7}$

5. $\dfrac{5}{6}$ $-\dfrac{2}{3}$

6. $\dfrac{1}{3}$ $-\dfrac{1}{12}$

7. $\dfrac{2}{4}$ $-\dfrac{1}{8}$

8. $\dfrac{1}{2}$ $-\dfrac{4}{10}$

9. $\dfrac{7}{9}$ $-\dfrac{11}{18}$

10. $\dfrac{5}{6}$ $-\dfrac{9}{12}$

11. $\dfrac{4}{8}$ $-\dfrac{1}{2}$

12. $\dfrac{1}{2}$ $-\dfrac{1}{4}$

13. $\dfrac{6}{8}$ $-\dfrac{1}{2}$

14. $\dfrac{3}{5}$ $-\dfrac{5}{10}$

15. $\dfrac{13}{14}$ $-\dfrac{6}{7}$

16. $\dfrac{3}{4}$ $-\dfrac{3}{8}$

Unit 6 Test

Fractions

Read the question. Use an extra piece of paper to write problems down and solve them. Fill in the circle beside the best answer.

☐ Example:

Convert the fraction to a mixed number in lowest terms.

$\frac{10}{4}$ $2\frac{2}{4}$ $3\frac{1}{2}$ $2\frac{4}{5}$ NG
     Ⓐ   Ⓑ   Ⓒ   Ⓓ

Read all the answer choices before you choose the one you think is correct.

Answer: D because the correct mixed number in lowest terms (2 ½) is not given.

Now try these. You have 20 minutes.

Continue until you see ⬡STOP .

1. Match the diagram with the fraction. $\frac{4}{8}$	Ⓐ	Ⓑ	Ⓒ	NG Ⓓ
2. Find the number. $\frac{1}{5}$ of 20	6 Ⓐ	5 Ⓑ	4 Ⓒ	10 Ⓓ
3. What is the equivalent fraction for $\frac{1}{2}$?	$\frac{3}{4}$ Ⓐ	$\frac{4}{8}$ Ⓑ	$\frac{5}{6}$ Ⓒ	$\frac{5}{11}$ Ⓓ
4. Reduce $\frac{10}{12}$ to lowest terms.	$\frac{5}{6}$ Ⓐ	$\frac{4}{8}$ Ⓑ	$\frac{5}{12}$ Ⓒ	$\frac{2}{6}$ Ⓓ

GO ON ➪

Unit 6 Test

5. Convert to a mixed number in lowest terms.

$\frac{9}{2}$

$5\frac{2}{9}$ Ⓐ $4\frac{1}{2}$ Ⓑ $4\frac{1}{9}$ Ⓒ $2\frac{1}{2}$ Ⓓ

6. Convert to a mixed number in lowest terms.

$\frac{13}{10}$

$1\frac{3}{10}$ Ⓐ $3\frac{1}{10}$ Ⓑ $2\frac{3}{10}$ Ⓒ NG Ⓓ

7. Add. Reduce to lowest terms.

$\frac{3}{12}$
$+ \frac{8}{12}$

$\frac{5}{12}$ Ⓐ $\frac{10}{12}$ Ⓑ $\frac{9}{10}$ Ⓒ $\frac{11}{12}$ Ⓓ

8. Subtract. Reduce to lowest terms.

$\frac{7}{14}$
$- \frac{2}{14}$

$\frac{2}{7}$ Ⓐ $\frac{5}{14}$ Ⓑ $\frac{3}{14}$ Ⓒ $\frac{9}{14}$ Ⓓ

9. Compare using >, <, or =.

$\frac{1}{8} \bigcirc \frac{3}{4}$

> Ⓐ < Ⓑ = Ⓒ NG Ⓓ

10. Add. Reduce to lowest terms.

$\frac{2}{7}$
$+ \frac{3}{14}$

$\frac{5}{14}$ Ⓐ $\frac{10}{14}$ Ⓑ $\frac{1}{2}$ Ⓒ $\frac{1}{14}$ Ⓓ

11. Subtract. Reduce to lowest terms.

$\frac{5}{8}$
$- \frac{2}{16}$

$\frac{1}{2}$ Ⓐ $\frac{9}{16}$ Ⓑ $\frac{3}{16}$ Ⓒ $\frac{3}{4}$ Ⓓ

GO ON

12. Match the equivalent fraction.

      Ⓐ   Ⓑ   Ⓒ   NG Ⓓ

13. Find the number.

$\frac{2}{7}$ of 14

4 Ⓐ   12 Ⓑ   2 Ⓒ   28 Ⓓ

14. Reduce to lowest terms.

$\frac{8}{10}$

$\frac{2}{4}$ Ⓐ $\frac{1}{2}$ Ⓑ $\frac{4}{6}$ Ⓒ $\frac{4}{5}$ Ⓓ

15. Convert to a mixed number in lowest terms.

$\frac{14}{3}$

$3\frac{5}{6}$ Ⓐ $4\frac{4}{6}$ Ⓑ $4\frac{2}{3}$ Ⓒ $3\frac{2}{3}$ Ⓓ

16. Add. Reduce to lowest terms.

$\frac{6}{12}$
$+ \frac{5}{12}$

$\frac{3}{4}$ Ⓐ $\frac{11}{12}$ Ⓑ $\frac{5}{6}$ Ⓒ   NG Ⓓ

17. Subtract. Reduce to lowest terms.

$\frac{14}{20}$
$- \frac{8}{20}$

$\frac{3}{10}$ Ⓐ $\frac{7}{20}$ Ⓑ $\frac{8}{20}$ Ⓒ $\frac{2}{5}$ Ⓓ

18. Compare using >, <, or =.

$\frac{3}{5}$ ◯ $\frac{4}{5}$

> Ⓐ   < Ⓑ   = Ⓒ   NG Ⓓ

GO ON

19. Add. Reduce to lowest terms.

$$\frac{1}{3}$$

$$+ \frac{4}{12}$$

$$\frac{9}{12}$$ **(A)**

$$\frac{2}{3}$$ **(B)**

$$\frac{5}{12}$$ **(C)**

NG **(D)**

20. Subtract. Reduce to lowest terms.

$$\frac{7}{8}$$

$$- \frac{3}{16}$$

$$\frac{11}{16}$$ **(A)**

$$\frac{4}{16}$$ **(B)**

$$\frac{4}{8}$$ **(C)**

$$1\frac{1}{16}$$ **(D)**

Explain why the two fractions below are equivalent.

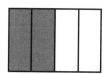 $\frac{2}{4}$

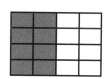 $\frac{8}{16}$

_____

_____

_____

_____

_____

Write two other fractions that are equivalent. Draw diagrams to explain.

STOP

Name

Telling time

Time can be told as:

A. Minutes after the hour—
   Start at the 12 and count
   the minutes after the hour.

B. Minutes before the hour—Start at the
   12 and count the minutes before the
   hour. *Tell time this way when it is
   more than 30 minutes past the hour.

20 minutes past 10
10:20

42 minutes after 10
10:42

50 minutes after 4
10 minutes before 5
4:50

40 minutes after 2
20 minutes before 3
2:40

Write the times.

1. ____ minutes

   after ____

2. ____ minutes

   after ____

3. ____ minutes

   after ____

4. ____ minutes

   after ____

5. ___ minutes after ___

   ___ minutes before ___

6. ___ minutes after ___

   ___ minutes before ___

7. ___ minutes after ___

   ___ minutes before ___

Figure the elapsed times.

8. Add 10
   minutes.

____:____

9. Add 20
   minutes.

____:____

10. Add 30
    minutes.

____:____

11. Add 15
    minutes.

____:____

Name

Using a calendar   Unit 7

There are 7 days in a week. Sunday is the first day of the week. There are 52 weeks
in a year. There are 12 months in a year. There are 365 $\frac{1}{4}$ days in a year.
$\frac{1}{4} + \frac{1}{4} + \frac{1}{4} + \frac{1}{4} = 1$ extra day—it is added to February during a leap year.
Every fourth year February has 29 days. February has 28 days in non-leap years.
April, June, September, and November have 30 days. January, March, May, July,
August, October, and December have 31 days.

Answer the questions using the calendar for March.

March						
S	M	T	W	Th	F	S
				1	2	3
4	5	6	7	8	9	10
11	12	13	14	15	16	17
18	19	20	21	22	23	24
25	26	27	28	29	30	31

1. The first of March is on what day?

   _____

2. What date in March is the first Sunday?

   _____

3. How many full weeks are there in March? _____

4. What day is 7 days after Monday, March 12th? _____

5. What day does the last day in March fall on? _____
   What is the date? _____

6. What day does March 22nd fall on? _____

7. What is the date for the last Tuesday in March? _____

Answer the questions using the calendar for July.

July						
S	M	T	W	Th	F	S
1	2	3	4	5	6	7
8	9	10	11	12	13	14
15	16	17	18	19	20	21
22	23	24	25	26	27	28
29	30	31				

8. What day does July 4th fall on?

   _____

9. What day does July 20th fall on?

   _____

10. What date does the last Tuesday in July fall on? _____

11. Thursday, the 19th of July, is how many weeks past the 5th of July? _____

12. What is the date of the third Sunday in July? _____

13. What day comes 4 days after Saturday, July 21st? _____

14. What is the date on the second Saturday in July? _____

Metric units of length

100 centimeters = 1 meter
100 cm = 1 m

1,000 meters = 1 kilometer
1,000 m = 1 km

1 centimeter (cm)

1 meter (m)

1 kilometer (km)

Choose the best unit to measure.

1. The length of your car.   A. cm   B. m   C. km

2. The distance from your house to your school.   A. cm   B. m   C. km

3. The length of your pencil.   A. cm   B. m   C. km

4. The distance from your house to the grocery store.   A. cm   B. m   C. km

5. The distance from your city to Washington, D.C.   A. cm   B. m   C. km

6. The length of a swimming pool.   A. cm   B. m   C. km

7. The length of your pinky finger.   A. cm   B. m   C. km

8. The height of a tree.   A. cm   B. m   C. km

9. The width of a quarter.   A. cm   B. m   C. km

10. The width of this book.   A. cm   B. m   C. km

Convert to complete the cross-number puzzle.
Include the unit in your answer.

Across

3. 8 km = _____ m

5. 10 km = _____ m

6. 5 m = _____ cm

8. 2 km = _____ m

9. 7 m = _____ cm

Down

1. 4 km = _____ m

2. 6 km = _____ m

4. 70 m = _____ cm

7. 9 km = _____ m

Name

Metric units of mass

Unit 7

1,000 grams = 1 kilogram

1,000 g = 1 kg

1 gram (g)

1 kilogram (kg)

Circle the correct unit to measure the following items.

1.

g   kg

2.

g   kg

3.

g   kg

4.

g   kg

5.

g   kg

6.

g   kg

7.

g   kg

Circle the best estimate.

8.

60 g   60 kg

9.

11 g   11 kg

10.

1 g   1 kg

11.

15 g   15 kg

12.

30 g   30 kg

13.

10 g   10 kg

14.

7 g   7 kg

Name

Metric units of capacity

1,000 millimeters = 1 liter

1,000 mL = 1 L

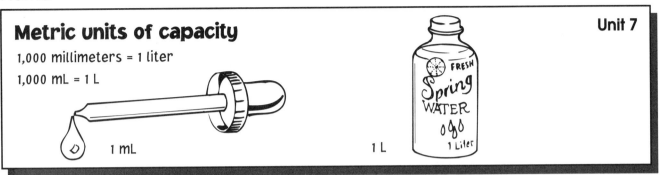

1 mL

1 L

Convert.

1. 5 L = _____ mL   2. 3 L = _____ mL   3. 8 L = _____ mL   4. 1 L = _____ mL

5. 7 L = _____ mL   6. 9 L = _____ mL   7. 2 L = _____ mL   8. 11 L = _____ mL

Circle the best estimate.

9.

500 mL   500 L

10.

20 mL   20 L

11.

1,000 mL   1,000 L

12.

15 mL   15 L

13.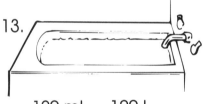

120 mL   120 L

14.

4 mL   4 L

15.

5 mL   5 L

16.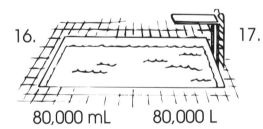

80,000 mL   80,000 L

17.

400 mL   400 L

18.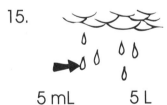

255 mL   255 L

19.

17 mL   17 L

20.

10 mL   10 L

Name

U.S. customary units of length

12 inches (in.) = 1 foot (ft.)
3 feet (ft.) = 1 yard (yd.)
5,280 feet (ft.) = 1 mile (mi.)
1,760 yards (yd.) = 1 mile (mi.)

1 in.  2 ft.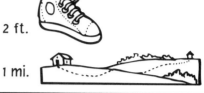

1 yd.   1 mi.

Measure the length to the nearest inch or half-inch.

1. _____ in. _____

2. _____ in. _____

3. _____ in. _____

4. _____ in. _____

5. _____ in. _____

6. _____ in. _____

Convert.

7. 3 ft. = _____ in.   8. 3 yd. = _____ ft.   9. 2 mi. = _____ yd.

10. 10 ft. = _____ in.   11. 4 mi. = _____ ft.   12. 5 yd. = _____ ft.

13. 8 ft. = _____ in.   14. 7 ft. = _____ in.   15. 10 yd. = _____ ft.

16. 1 mi. = _____ ft.   17. 2 yd. = _____ ft.   18. 6 yd. = _____ ft.

Circle the most appropriate unit of measure.

19.

in.   yd.

20.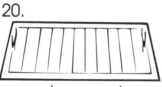

in.   yd.

21.

in.   mi.

22.

yd.   mi.

23.

mi.   yd.

24.

ft.   yd.

25.

in.   ft.

26.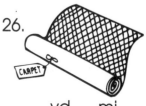

yd.   mi.

Name _____

U.S. customary units of capacity and weight   Unit 7

2 cups (c.) = 1 pint (pt.)
2 pints = 1 quart (qt.)
4 quarts = 1 gallon (gal.)
16 ounces (oz.) = 1 pound (lb.)
2,000 pounds = 1 ton (t.)

1 oz.

1 lb.   1 t.

Compare the units of measurement using **>**, **<**, or **=**.

1. 14 oz. ◯ 1 lb.   2. 4 c. ◯ 1 pt.   3. 2 qt. ◯ 2 pt.

4. 3 gal. ◯ 12 qt.   5. 1 qt. ◯ 3 pt.   6. 3 lb. ◯ 32 oz.

7. 2 t. ◯ 3,000 lb.   8. 4 c. ◯ 2 pt.   9. 1 t. ◯ 2,000 lb.

10. 2 c. ◯ 2 pt.   11. 3 qt. ◯ 1 gal.   12. 2 lb. ◯ 30 oz.

13. 8 qt. ◯ 3 gal.   14. 17 oz. ◯ 1 lb.   15. 1 qt. ◯ 4 pt.

Circle the most appropriate unit of measure.

16. 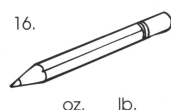   17. 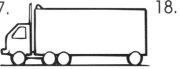   18.    19.

oz.   lb.   lb.   t.   c.   gal.   oz.   lb.

20.    21. 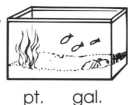   22.    23.

c.   qt.   pt.   gal.   oz.   lb.   c.   gal.

Convert.

24. 3 lb. = _____ oz.   25. 2 t. = _____ lb.   26. 2 gal. = _____ qt.

27. 2 qt. = _____ pt.   28. 3 pt. = _____ c.   29. 3 qt. = _____ pt.

30. 5 lb. = _____ oz.   31. 5 qt. = _____ pt.   32. 8 gal. = _____ qt.

Teach & Test Math: Grade 4

Name

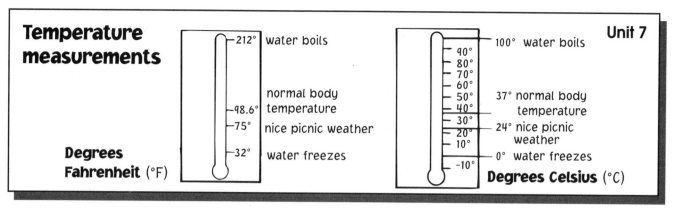

Temperature measurements

Degrees Fahrenheit (°F)

- 212° water boils
- 98.6° normal body temperature
- 75° nice picnic weather
- 32° water freezes

- 100° water boils
- 40°
- 80°
- 70°
- 60°
- 50°
- 37° normal body temperature
- 40°
- 30° 24° nice picnic weather
- 20°
- 10°
- 0° water freezes
- –10°

Degrees Celsius (°C)

Unit 7

Write the temperatures.

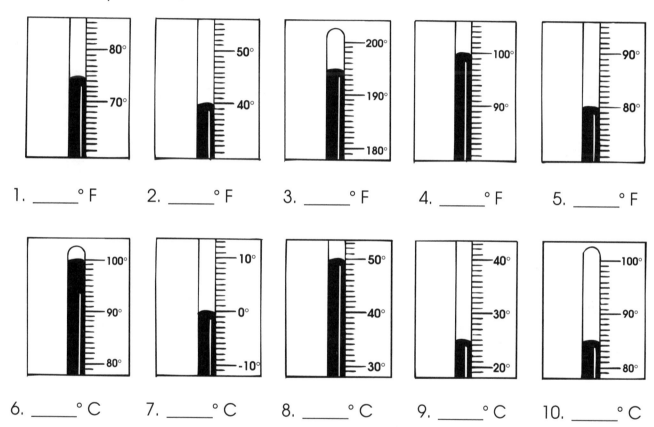

1. _____° F

2. _____° F

3. _____° F

4. _____° F

5. _____° F

6. _____° C

7. _____° C

8. _____° C

9. _____° C

10. _____° C

Match the temperatures. (°C and °F).

11. Playing in the snow _____ _____

12. Water boiling _____ _____

13. Normal body temperature _____ _____

14. A nice day for a picnic _____ _____

15. Water freezing _____ _____

A. 32° F   F. 100° C

B. 98.6° F   G. 75° F

C. 212° F   H. 0° C

D. 37° C   I. 24° C

E. 28° F   J. -2° C

Name

Pictographs and bar graphs

Pictographs use pictures to compare information.

Each ★ stands for 2 awards.

Good Deed Awards

Mark	★ ★ ★ ★
Gwen	★ ★ ★ ★ ★
Emily	★ ★
Katie	★
Billy	★ ★ ★

Bar graphs use bars to compare information.

Favorite Fruit

Use the graphs to answer each question.

Lindy Elementary Food Drive

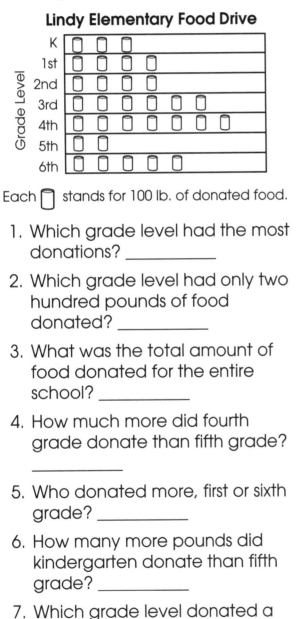

Each ⬭ stands for 100 lb. of donated food.

1. Which grade level had the most donations? _____

2. Which grade level had only two hundred pounds of food donated? _____

3. What was the total amount of food donated for the entire school? _____

4. How much more did fourth grade donate than fifth grade? _____

5. Who donated more, first or sixth grade? _____

6. How many more pounds did kindergarten donate than fifth grade? _____

7. Which grade level donated a total of five hundred pounds? _____

Rocket Day Fun!

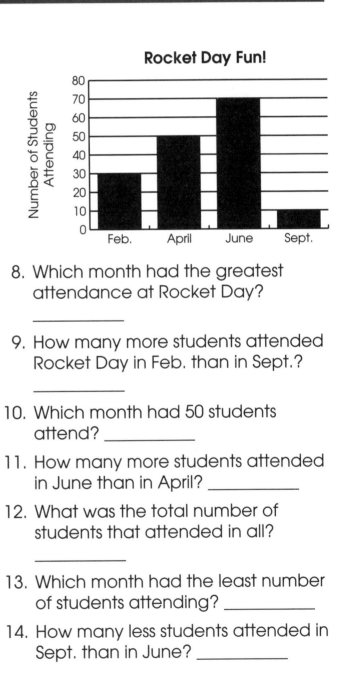

8. Which month had the greatest attendance at Rocket Day? _____

9. How many more students attended Rocket Day in Feb. than in Sept.? _____

10. Which month had 50 students attend? _____

11. How many more students attended in June than in April? _____

12. What was the total number of students that attended in all? _____

13. Which month had the least number of students attending? _____

14. How many less students attended in Sept. than in June? _____

Circle graphs and line graphs

Circle graphs are divided into parts to display facts.

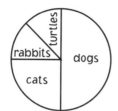

Line graphs are used to show change.

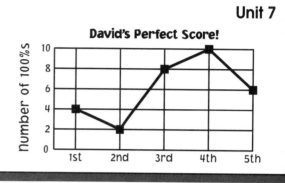

Use the graphs to answer each question.

Favorite Vegetables

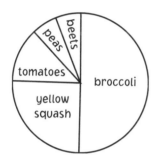

1. Which two vegetables are the least favorite? _____

2. Which is the favorite vegetable? _____

3. Which vegetable is liked half as much as broccoli? _____

4. Which vegetable is liked more, peas or tomatoes? _____

5. Which vegetable is liked twice as much as yellow squash? _____

6. Which vegetable is liked twice as much as tomatoes? _____

7. Which vegetable is as popular as all the other vegetables combined? _____

Baby-sitting Jobs

8. Which month was Eva called for the most baby-sitting jobs? _____

9. Between which two months was the greatest decrease in calls to baby-sit? _____

10. Between which two months was the greatest increase in baby-sitting jobs? _____

11. What was the total number of baby-sitting jobs between October and December? _____

12. Which two months tied for the least number of baby-sitting jobs? _____

13. What was the total number of baby-sitting jobs for the months displayed? _____

Unit 7 Test

Measurement, Graphs

Read the question. Use an extra piece of paper to write problems down and solve them. Fill in the circle beside the best answer.

Take time to review your answers.

 Example:

What time will it be in 10 minutes?

1:55   7:05   7:15   NG
(A)   (B)   (C)   (D)

Answer: C because 10 minutes of elapsed time added to 7:05 will be 7:15.

Now try these. You have 20 minutes. Continue until you see (STOP).

---

1. Tell the time.

    7:30   6:15   3:30   7:15
    (A)   (B)   (C)   (D)

---

2. What time will it be in 25 minutes?

    3:00   7:05   2:55   2:35
    (A)   (B)   (C)   (D)

Use the calendar for the month of January to answer questions 3–5.

January						
S	M	T	W	Th	F	S
	1	2	3	4	5	6
7	8	9	10	11	12	13
14	15	16	17	18	19	20
21	22	23	24	25	26	27
28	29	30	31			

GO ON

3. What is the date on the first Wednesday of January?

4	10	2	NG
Ⓐ	Ⓑ	Ⓒ	Ⓓ

4. On which day does the 15th of January fall?

Monday	Sunday	Tuesday	Wednesday
Ⓐ	Ⓑ	Ⓒ	Ⓓ

5. The 22nd of January falls on what day?

Friday	Saturday	Monday	Tuesday
Ⓐ	Ⓑ	Ⓒ	Ⓓ

Choose the most appropriate unit of measurement for questions 6–12.

6. the length of your house

km	cm	m	g
Ⓐ	Ⓑ	Ⓒ	Ⓓ

7. the length of your pencil

m	cm	kg	km
Ⓐ	Ⓑ	Ⓒ	Ⓓ

8. the distance from your house to the grocery store

cm	m	mL	NG
Ⓐ	Ⓑ	Ⓒ	Ⓓ

9. the mass of a dime

kg	g	cm	km
Ⓐ	Ⓑ	Ⓒ	Ⓓ

GO ON ▷

10. the mass of your shoes

    g   cm   kg   mL
  Ⓐ   Ⓑ   Ⓒ   Ⓓ

11. the capacity of a water bottle

    mL   L   cm   km
  Ⓐ   Ⓑ   Ⓒ   Ⓓ

12. the capacity of a raindrop

    L   mL   kg   NG
  Ⓐ   Ⓑ   Ⓒ   Ⓓ

Convert the following measurements.

13. 2 ft. = _____ in.

    36   12   27   24
  Ⓐ   Ⓑ   Ⓒ   Ⓓ

14. 2 yd. = _____ ft.

    10   6   4   36
  Ⓐ   Ⓑ   Ⓒ   Ⓓ

15. 5,280 ft. = _____ mi.

    3   5   1   NG
  Ⓐ   Ⓑ   Ⓒ   Ⓓ

16. 8 qt. = _____ gal.

    2   6   8   4
  Ⓐ   Ⓑ   Ⓒ   Ⓓ

17. Tell the temperature in degrees Fahrenheit.

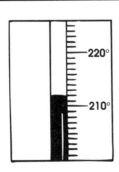

    230° F   212° F   202° F   210° F
     Ⓐ   Ⓑ   Ⓒ   Ⓓ

GO ON

Use the graphs to answer questions 18–20.

18. What is the total number of votes for favorite color?

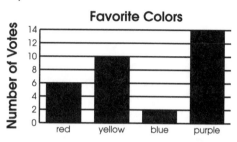

Favorite Colors

(A) 16   (B) 32

(C) 41   (D) 26

19. What is the difference in growth from January to July?

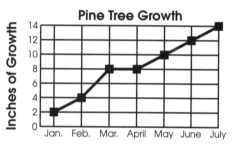

Pine Tree Growth

(A) 15 in.   (B) 25 in.

(C) 12 in.   (D) 14 in.

20. What is the most popular sandwich?

Popular Sandwiches

(A) salami   (B) turkey

(C) cheese   (D) NG

Create a bar graph representing pet ownership. Pretend students in your class own a total of 6 rabbits, 12 cats, 14 dogs, and 2 birds.

Write two questions that can be answered using your completed graph.

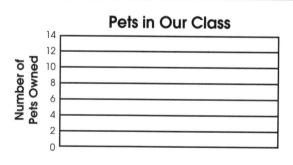

Pets in Our Class

Choosing the operation

Look for key words when deciding which operation to use. Here are a few examples of what to look for:

Addition: How many are there in all, or altogether? Example: Teddy built 5 ship models. Bill built 4. How many do they have altogether?

Subtraction: How many were left, or leftover, or remaining? What is the difference? Example: They started out with 200 books. They sold 140. How many are remaining?

Multiplication: Look for the total of multiple groups. Example: The price for one ticket for the music festival is $2.00. What will 4 tickets cost? What will be the price for 7 tickets?

Division: Look for the total given, and the question asking for how many in each group. Example: If the total is 400, and there are 5 groups, how many are there in each group?

Write which operation is to be used in each problem. Solve.

1. Albert has volunteered 3 Saturdays this month at the food bank. Eddie has volunteered 4. Lenny is really excited about helping others! He has volunteered 5 times! What is the total number of Saturdays these boys have volunteered to help out at the food bank?

   Operation: _____   Answer: _____

2. This week, 27 girls signed up for ballet class. Last week, 16 girls signed up. How many more signed up this week?

   Operation: _____   Answer: _____

3. A total of 200 students showed up for the bike rodeo on Saturday! Each of the 5 volunteers checked the same number of bikes to make sure they were safe. How many bikes did each volunteer check?

   Operation: _____   Answer: _____

4. Mr. Schnoodles was dunked 5 times by each of the 3 students that stepped up to see him plunge into the freezing cold water at the carnival! How many times was Mr. Schnoodles dunked in all?

   Operation: _____   Answer: _____

5. The carnival needed cakes for the cake walk. The 3rd grade brought 12, the 4th grade brought 23, and the 5th grade brought 14. How many cakes were brought in all?

   Operation: _____   Answer: _____

6. There are 6 magnifying lenses in each bag. Mrs. Pickles took out 7 bags so that each student could have one. How many lenses did she take out in all?

   Operation: _____   Answer: _____

Name

Using a tree diagram   Unit 8

Tammy and Debbie love potatoes. The restaurant where they are gives a choice of a red potato or a brown potato. Also, it is served three different ways: mashed, baked, or as French fries! How many different choices are there? To find out, use a tree diagram.

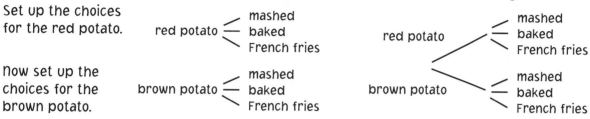

Set up the choices for the red potato.

Now set up the choices for the brown potato.

How many choices do we have altogether? Three choices for the red potato, and 3 choices for the brown. That's a total of 6 different choices.

Solve each problem. Use a tree diagram.

1. David wants to buy a brand new bike. He has a choice of a mountain, road, or BMX bike. The store has each of these bikes in a choice of red, blue, or purple. How many choices does he have in all?

2. Eva and four of her friends are at the school picnic together. They have decided to get something to eat. They have a choice between a hot dog or a hamburger. How many choices are there between all 5 friends?

3. Monica wants to buy a new binder for school. The store where she is has a choice between 1½ in. or 2 in. width binders. Each of these come in red, blue, black, green or brown. How many choices does she have in all?

4. Mark loves fruit! He is at the grocery store with his mom, and she says that she will buy for him either apples or grapes. They each come in red or green. How many choices does Mark have altogether?

5. Marlene's class divides into 5 lab groups for science. Each group today has to decide what type of plant they are going to grow for their science experiment. They can choose either lima beans, string beans, yellow squash, corn, or watermelon. Within all 5 groups, how many choices can be made altogether?

Using a table   Unit 8

Tables are helpful in organizing information.

Sam's Market

Today's Fruit Prices	No tax on food.
Fresh Cherries	$2.99 per lb.
Red Delicious Apples	$.89 per lb.
Green Grapes	$1.49 per lb.
Strawberries	$3.49 per basket
Bananas	$.59 per lb.
Pineapples	$1.99 each

Use the information in the table to answer the questions.

1. Jose wants to buy 1 pound of grapes and a pineapple.
   He only has $5.00. Can he purchase these two items? _____

2. The cherries look so good! Tammy wants to buy
   3 pounds. What will her total cost be? _____

3. Gwen is planning on making a delicious fruit salad.
   She still needs a basket of strawberries, a pineapple,
   and a pound of fresh cherries. What will her total cost be? _____

4. Alecia wants to buy two different types of fruit, but she is trying very hard to
   save money. Which would be less expensive, a basket of strawberries and a
   pound of bananas, or a pound of fresh cherries and a pound of green
   grapes? _____

5. Anna just bought 3 pounds of one type of fruit at Sam's Market. She spent a
   total of $4.47. Looking at the chart, what type of fruit did she buy? _____

6. David wants to purchase a pound of Red Delicious apples and a pound of
   bananas. What will he pay altogether? _____

7. Andy has 6 quarters. Does he have enough money to purchase a
   pineapple? _____

Name

Anthony and his scout troop hiked 2 miles and then rested. After their break, they hiked another 3 miles. The total distance of the hike was 7 miles. How many more miles did they need to go before reaching their destination?

Step one: Add the total distance hiked so far. 2 + 3 = 5

Step two: Subtract this sum from the total to find the remaining difference. 7 − 5 = 2

Answer: They must hike 2 more miles to reach their destination.

Use two or more steps to solve each problem.

1. Lupe and Mary have each blown up 4 balloons. They need a total of 20 balloons for the party at school. How many more do they need to blow up?

2. Lee has collected a total of 29 cans and boxes of food for the food drive. Chung has collected 27. Their team goal was to collect 75 cans of food altogether. How many more do they need to collect to reach their awesome goal?

3. Yesterday, Eric picked 134 apples off the tree in his backyard. Today, he picked another 166 apples. His father asked him to divide the total in half so that they could share their apples with the food bank. How many apples did they donate?

4. Roger, Heather, and Max each raised $3.00 for the fund-raiser at school by selling pretzels at the carnival. They need a total of $15.00 to reach their goal. How much more do they need to raise to reach their goal?

5. Walter pays $2.00 each time he goes to the water park to swim. He has already been there 5 times this summer! How many more times will he go before he spends a total of $20.00?

6. Zippora loves to draw! She is so good that people are willing to pay $5.00 for her drawings. She has sold 10 drawings so far. How many more will she have to sell to earn a total of $75.00?

Name

Too much information   Unit 8

1. Figure out which information is necessary to solve the problem.
2. Determine the operation.
3. Write a number sentence.
4. Solve.

Andy brought 7 songs to play on guitar. Bill brought 6. They both brought 4 songs for the piano. How many songs did they bring in all for the guitar?

Needed information: Total songs brought for the guitar.
Operation: Addition
Number sentence: 7 + 6 =
Answer: 13 songs

Solve.

1. Mr. Smiley asked his fourth-grade class how many of them owned kittens. He was amazed to find out that everyone raised their hands! The total amount was 44! Upon asking, he also found out that 25 dogs resided at these same homes! If there are 2 kittens per household, how many students are there in Mr. Smiley's class?

Needed information:

Operation:

Number sentence:

Answer:

2. A total of 356 pounds of paper were collected for recycling by Mrs. Wick's class in the last four weeks. 289 pounds of cardboard were also collected. What is the average number of pounds of paper collected each week?

3. The Hot Dog Barn was running a special. Hot dogs were only $.49 on Wednesdays. Hamburgers were $.89. Mr. Harland ordered 9 hot dogs for the students that did extra credit on their homework. How much did he pay for the hot dogs?

4. Maria's class has 4 pet mice in their classroom that they love to play with every day. They also have 2 hamsters. Each of the mice had 10 babies. How many mice does the class have now?

5. Forty students at Armstrong Elementary School joined choir the first week of school. Fifty students joined the band. The second week, 25 more students joined the choir. What was the total number of students that joined the choir?

Name

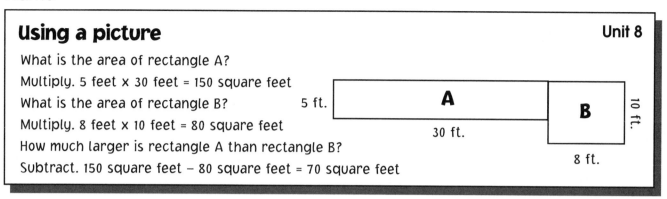

What is the area of rectangle A?

Multiply. 5 feet x 30 feet = 150 square feet

What is the area of rectangle B?

Multiply. 8 feet x 10 feet = 80 square feet

How much larger is rectangle A than rectangle B?

Subtract. 150 square feet – 80 square feet = 70 square feet

Use the picture below to answer the questions about the Wong Family's upstairs.

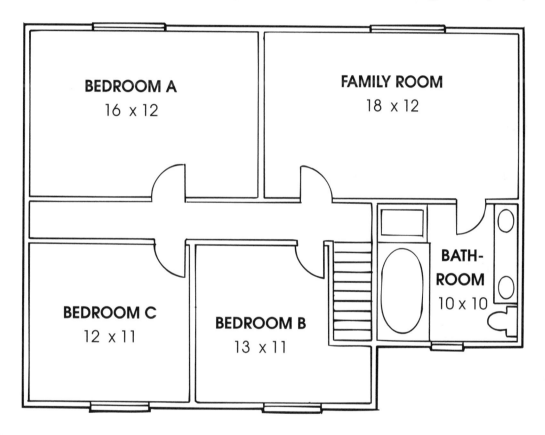

1. What is the area of the family room? _____ sq. ft.

2. How much larger is the family room than bedroom C? _____ sq. ft.

3. How many square feet do the three bedrooms total? _____ sq. ft.

4. What is the square footage of the bathroom? _____ sq. ft.

5. What is the total square footage of the entire upstairs? _____ sq. ft.

6. What is the difference in size between the largest bedroom and the
   bathroom? _____ sq. ft.

Name

Using a pattern

The best way to understand a pattern is to look at the difference between each number.
Is there a pattern that follows all the numbers within the group?

Examples:

A. 7, 5, 3, 1 The pattern takes away 2 as it goes downward until it reaches 1.

B. 3, 7, 11, 15 The pattern adds 4 to each additional number.

Solve each problem. Identify the pattern.

1. On Monday, Mr. Newland gave out 3 problems for homework. Tuesday, he gave out 8 problems. On Wednesday, he assigned 13 problems! How many problems did he assign for Thursday and Friday?

2. Thomas loves to share. On the first field day he gave out 1 water bottle. The second day, he shared 3 bottles. The third day, he gave out 5 extra bottles of water. How many did he share on the fourth day if he continues this pattern?

3. The first week of the school fund-raiser Jacelyn sold 5 gifts. The second week, she sold 11 gifts. The third week, she sold 17! If this pattern continues, how many gifts will she sell the fifth week?

4. Monica ran the mile during P.E. and had a time of 8 minutes and 10 seconds. The second week she ran, her time was 7 minutes and 50 seconds. The third week, she improved her time to 7 minutes and 30 seconds. If she was able to keep up this pattern, what will her next time be for running the mile?

5. Mrs. Kliesen and Mr. Primm teamed up to have an after-school math club. The first week, only 1 person showed up for the club. The second week, 3 people showed up. The third week, 9 people showed up. How many students showed up the fourth week?

6. Angelica loves her puppy. Each day she gives him 2 puppy treats while she is training him. If there are a total of 20 treats in the box, how many days will these last?

7. Andy loves to eat dates. He eats a few every day for lunch. The box started out with a total of 36. After the first day of lunch there were 31 remaining. After the second day there were 26. Continuing this same pattern, how many is he eating each day?

Name

Classifying   Unit 8

The words all, some, no, or none can be used when comparing. Examples:

All dogs are animals.   All addition problems use the addition (+) sign.
Some animals are dogs.   Some math problems use the addition sign.
No cats are dogs.   No division problems use the addition sign.

Complete each statement with **all**, **some**, **no**, or **none**.

1. _____ rectangles have 4 vertices. _____ rectangles are
   parallelograms. _____ rectangles are circles.

2. _____ even numbers end in "0." _____ even numbers end in
   an even number. _____ even number ends with an odd number.

3. _____ addition problems have an answer called a "sum."
   _____ addition problems have an answer called a "difference."
   _____ math problems have an answer called a "sum."

4. _____ math problems multiply factors. _____ multiplication
   problems multiply 2 or more factors. _____ subtraction problems
   multiply factors.

5. _____ triangles have 4 vertices. _____ triangles are congruent.
   _____ triangles have 3 vertices.

Look at the diagrams to complete the statements using **all**, **some**, or **none**.

6. _____ of the polygons in this diagram have less than 3 vertices.

7. _____ polygons are congruent.

8. _____ polygons have three or more sides.

Name

Read the question. Use an extra piece of paper to write problems down and solve them. Fill in the circle beside the best answer.

☐ Example:

Choose the operation.

Alex has a total of 56 different seashells. He wants to give each of his 8 friends the same amount. How many will each friend receive?

(A) addition
(B) division
(C) multiplication
(D) NG

Note the time allotment. Pace yourself.

Answer: B because you must divide in order to find out what equal amounts you can give out.

Now try these. You have 20 minutes. Continue until you see STOP.

For problems 1–3, choose the operation.

1. Live turtles cost $1.59 each. Cal wants to buy 4. How much will he spend?

multiplication	subtraction	addition	division
(A)	(B)	(C)	(D)

2. Carolyn has sold snowcones 3 times this summer. The first time she sold 27. The second time she sold 41, and the third time she sold 39. How many did she sell in all?

subtraction	division	addition	multiplication
(A)	(B)	(C)	(D)

3. Mark is allowed 300 minutes each week on his computer using the internet. So far he has used up 138 minutes. How many minutes does he have left?

multiplication	division	addition	NG
(A)	(B)	(C)	(D)

GO ON ➡

4. Katelyn can either get red or black shoes. She also has a choice between running, hiking, or regular walking shoes. How many choices does she have in all?

   10   5   6   3
   Ⓐ   Ⓑ   Ⓒ   Ⓓ

5. Allyn is looking at the menu. He has a choice between soup, salad, or cornbread to go along with his entree. There are three types of soup, three types of salad, and three types of cornbread. How many choices does he really have?

   6   9   24   12
   Ⓐ   Ⓑ   Ⓒ   Ⓓ

6. Kimberly is amazed! There are 5 different drinks to choose from. And to top that off, each one can be served hot or cold. How many choices does Kimberly have in all?

   10   7   4   NG
   Ⓐ   Ⓑ   Ⓒ   Ⓓ

7. Cheryl has completed 7 hours of community service, and Jim has completed 9 hours. Together they must complete a total of 20 hours. How many more hours do they have to complete to reach their goal?

   6 hours   5 hours   4 hours   16 hours
   Ⓐ   Ⓑ   Ⓒ   Ⓓ

Use the chart to answer questions 8–10.

Plant Growth Chart

	1st Week	3rd Week	5th Week
Corn	2 in.	5 in.	8 in.
Sunflowers	1 in.	6 in.	10 in.
Tomatoes	2 in.	4 in.	7 in.

GO ON

8. Which plant grew the tallest after 5 weeks?

tomatoes   sunflowers   corn   NG
(A)   (B)   (C)   (D)

9. Order the plants from shortest to tallest.

(A) sunflowers, corn, tomatoes   (B) tomatoes, corn, sunflowers

(C) corn, sunflowers, tomatoes   (D) tomatoes, sunflowers, corn

10. What is the total number of inches grown for all the plants combined after 5 weeks?

45 inches   30 inches   25 inches   35 inches
(A)   (B)   (C)   (D)

11. Erica earns $4.00 every time she baby-sits. She has already baby-sat 5 times. She needs to earn a total of $24.00 for a gift she wants to buy her dad. How many more times does she need to baby-sit to buy this gift?

1 time   4 times   3 times   2 times
(A)   (B)   (C)   (D)

12. Aaron practiced 4 hours this week on his violin. Last week, he practiced 3 hours on the violin and 2 hours on the piano. How many more hours did he practice the violin this week?

2 hours   1 hour   3 hours   NG
(A)   (B)   (C)   (D)

13. Ty and Ed built a model sailing ship together. It had a total of 546 pieces! A car that they built had only 321 pieces. If each of them put together equal amounts of the ship, how many pieces did they each put together?

273 pieces   321 pieces   250 pieces   867 pieces
(A)   (B)   (C)   (D)

GO ON ▷

Use the diagram to answer questions 14–16.

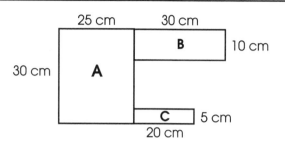

14. What is the total square area of all three rectangles?

    1,240 sq. cm   1,000 sq. cm   1,150 sq. cm   1,200 sq. cm
       Ⓐ   Ⓑ   Ⓒ   Ⓓ

15. How much larger is rectangle A than rectangle B?

    200 sq. cm   500 sq. cm   425 sq. cm   450 sq. cm
      Ⓐ   Ⓑ   Ⓒ   Ⓓ

16. How many times larger is rectangle B than rectangle C?

      6   4   3   NG
      Ⓐ   Ⓑ   Ⓒ   Ⓓ

17. Elisha rode his bike to school 5 times in March. In April, he rode his bike to school 10 times. In May, he rode his bike to school 15 times. If there was school in June, how many times would he have ridden his bike to school to continue this pattern?

    20 times   25 times   21 times   15 times
      Ⓐ   Ⓑ   Ⓒ   Ⓓ

18. Dick and Joan love to travel. Their mom and dad took them on 3 trips last year. This year they plan to go on 5 trips. And, next year, they plan to go on 7 trips! How many trips will they go on the year after that if they keep up the same pattern?

    8 trips   4 trips   10 trips   NG
     Ⓐ   Ⓑ   Ⓒ   Ⓓ

GO ON ▷

Complete the following statements.

19. _____ math problems contain an answer called a "product."

All	Some	No	None
Ⓐ	Ⓑ	Ⓒ	Ⓓ

20. _____ division problems contain an answer called a "quotient."

All	Some	No	None
Ⓐ	Ⓑ	Ⓒ	Ⓓ

Draw a tree diagram for the following problem.

Earl is looking for a puppy. The pet store has Golden Retrievers, Dalmatians, and St. Bernards. There are 4 of each breeds from which to choose. How many choices does Earl have?

Why did you draw your diagram this way? _____

_____

Does your diagram support the answer you have given? _____

_____

_____

Final Review Test Name Grid

Write your name in pencil in the boxes along the top. Begin with your last name. Fill in as many letters as will fit. Then follow the columns straight down and bubble in the letters that correspond with the letters in your name. Complete the rest of the information the same way. You may use a piece of scrap paper to help you keep your place.

STUDENT'S NAME			SCHOOL
LAST	FIRST	MI	TEACHER

FEMALE ○   MALE ○

DATE OF BIRTH

MONTH	DAY	YEAR

The name grid contains columns of bubbled letters A–Z for LAST, FIRST, and MI.

DATE OF BIRTH bubbles:

MONTH	DAY	YEAR
JAN ○	⓪ ⓪	⓪ ⓪
FEB ○	① ①	① ①
MAR ○	② ②	② ②
APR ○	③ ③	③ ③
MAY ○	④	④ ④
JUN ○	⑤	⑤ ⑤
JUL ○	⑥	⑥ ⑥
AUG ○	⑦	⑦ ⑦
SEP ○	⑧	⑧ ⑧
OCT ○	⑨	⑨ ⑨
NOV ○		
DEC ○		

GRADE ③ ④ ⑤

Final Review Test Answer Sheet

Pay close attention when transferring your answers. Fill in the bubbles neatly and completely. You may use a piece of scrap paper to help you keep your place.

SAMPLES
A Ⓐ Ⓑ ● Ⓓ
B Ⓕ ● Ⓗ Ⓙ

1 Ⓐ Ⓑ Ⓒ Ⓓ	7 Ⓐ Ⓑ Ⓒ Ⓓ	13 Ⓐ Ⓑ Ⓒ Ⓓ	19 Ⓐ Ⓑ Ⓒ Ⓓ	25 Ⓐ Ⓑ Ⓒ Ⓓ
2 Ⓕ Ⓖ Ⓗ Ⓙ	8 Ⓕ Ⓖ Ⓗ Ⓙ	14 Ⓕ Ⓖ Ⓗ Ⓙ	20 Ⓕ Ⓖ Ⓗ Ⓙ	26 Ⓕ Ⓖ Ⓗ Ⓙ
3 Ⓐ Ⓑ Ⓒ Ⓓ	9 Ⓐ Ⓑ Ⓒ Ⓓ	15 Ⓐ Ⓑ Ⓒ Ⓓ	21 Ⓐ Ⓑ Ⓒ Ⓓ	27 Ⓐ Ⓑ Ⓒ Ⓓ
4 Ⓕ Ⓖ Ⓗ Ⓙ	10 Ⓕ Ⓖ Ⓗ Ⓙ	16 Ⓕ Ⓖ Ⓗ Ⓙ	22 Ⓕ Ⓖ Ⓗ Ⓙ	28 Ⓕ Ⓖ Ⓗ Ⓙ
5 Ⓐ Ⓑ Ⓒ Ⓓ	11 Ⓐ Ⓑ Ⓒ Ⓓ	17 Ⓐ Ⓑ Ⓒ Ⓓ	23 Ⓐ Ⓑ Ⓒ Ⓓ	29 Ⓐ Ⓑ Ⓒ Ⓓ
6 Ⓕ Ⓖ Ⓗ Ⓙ	12 Ⓕ Ⓖ Ⓗ Ⓙ	18 Ⓕ Ⓖ Ⓗ Ⓙ	24 Ⓕ Ⓖ Ⓗ Ⓙ	30 Ⓕ Ⓖ Ⓗ Ⓙ

Read the question. Use an extra piece of paper to work on problems and keep your place on the score sheet. Fill in the circle beside the best answer.

☐ Example:

Describe how these two lines relate to each other.

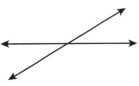

(A) parallel lines

(B) perpendicular lines

(C) intersecting lines

(D) NG

Answer: C because the two lines intersect.

Now try these. You have 30 minutes.

Continue until you see (STOP).

Remember your Helping Hand Strategies:

 1. Cross out answers you know are wrong.

 2. Read all the answer choices before you choose the one you think is correct.

 3. Take time to review your answers.

 4. Note the time allotment. Pace yourself.

 5. Transfer your answers carefully. Use a piece of scratch paper to keep your place on the answer sheet.

---

1. (16 − 8) + 4 = _____

14	12	17	20
(A)	(B)	(C)	(D)

---

2. Round 572 to the nearest hundred.

500	700	600	580
(F)	(G)	(H)	(J)

3.

$42.18
x   6

$300.60	$243.09	$421.62	$253.08
(A)	(B)	(C)	(D)

GO ON

Final Review Test

4.

$$\begin{array}{r} 287 \\ \times\ 32 \\ \hline \end{array}$$

7,822 (F)   1,948 (G)   9,184 (H)   1,435 (J)

5.

$6\overline{)56}$

9 R2 (A)   8 R8 (B)   9 R5 (C)   8 R4 (D)

6.

$9\overline{)279}$

54 (F)   42 (G)   31 (H)   NG (J)

7.

$4\overline{)927}$

231 R3 (A)   246 R1 (B)   231 R4 (C)   213 R3 (D)

8. Complete this set of decimals.

4.10, 4.11, _____, _____, _____

(F) 4.22, 4.33, 4.44   (G) 4.31, 4.41, 4.51

(H) 4.111, 4.1111, 4.11111   (J) NG

9. Round 3.89 to the nearest whole number.

3 (A)   4 (B)   6 (C)   3.9 (D)

GO ON

10.

$$
\begin{array}{r}
8.4 \\
-\ 2.26 \\
\end{array}
$$

6.26
(F)

5.46
(G)

6.14
(H)

10.66
(J)

11. Identify.

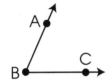

obtuse angle
(A)

right angle
(B)

vertex
(C)

acute angle
(D)

12. Identify the letter on the grid with the coordinates (2, 3).

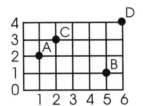

(F) B

(G) D

(H) A

(J) C

13. How do these two figures relate to each other?

(A) congruent

(B) similar

(C) rectangles

(D) NG

14. Find the volume.

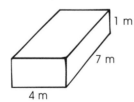

1 m
7 m
4 m

(F) 12 cu. cm

(G) 11 cu. cm

(H) 28 cu. cm

(J) 29 cu. cm

15. Identify this solid figure.

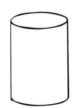

(A) rectangular prism

(B) cone

(C) cylinder

(D) pyramid

GO ON

Name

16. Identify the fraction of the shaded part. Reduce to lowest terms.

Ⓕ $\frac{2}{5}$ Ⓖ $\frac{4}{6}$

Ⓗ $\frac{4}{8}$ Ⓙ NG

17. Convert to a mixed number in lowest terms.

$\frac{22}{5}$

$6\frac{1}{5}$ Ⓐ $4\frac{2}{5}$ Ⓑ $2\frac{2}{5}$ Ⓒ $4\frac{1}{5}$ Ⓓ

18. Compare using >, <, or =.

$\frac{3}{7}$ ◯ $\frac{5}{7}$

$>$ Ⓕ $<$ Ⓖ $=$ Ⓗ   NG Ⓙ

19. Add. Reduce to lowest terms.

$\frac{1}{3}$
$+ \frac{2}{6}$

$\frac{3}{6}$ Ⓐ $\frac{5}{6}$ Ⓑ $\frac{2}{3}$ Ⓒ $\frac{4}{6}$ Ⓓ

20. Subtract. Reduce to lowest terms.

$\frac{8}{12}$
$- \frac{1}{6}$

$\frac{7}{12}$ Ⓕ $\frac{1}{2}$ Ⓖ $\frac{5}{6}$ Ⓗ $\frac{2}{3}$ Ⓙ

21. What will be the time in 20 minutes?

2:10 Ⓐ   2:45 Ⓑ   3:00 Ⓒ   2:25 Ⓓ

GO ON ▷

Choose the best unit of measurement for questions 22 and 23.

22. the width of this test

centimeters (cm)　　kilometers (km)　　meters (m)　　grams (g)
(F)　　　　　　　　(G)　　　　　　(H)　　　　　(J)

23. the mass of this book

grams (g)　　kilograms (kg)　　liters (L)　　meters (m)
(A)　　　　　　(B)　　　　　(C)　　　　(D)

24. Compare using >, <, or =.

1 gal ◯ 3 qt

= (F)　　　　> (G)　　　　< (H)　　　　NG (J)

Use the graph to answer the question.

25. What is the difference in inches of rainfall for October and February?

(A) 6 in.　　(B) 2 in.

(C) 4 in.　　(D) 8 in.

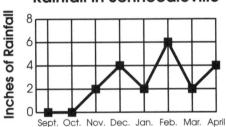

Rainfall in Schnoodleville

26. Identify the correct tree diagram for the following problem.

Roger can get a red sport's cap or a blue one. The red caps have a choice between 4 different football teams. The blue caps have a choice between 4 different baseball teams. How many choices does Roger have altogether?

(F)

(G)

(H)

NG
(J)

GO ON

Teach & Test Math: Grade 4

27. Choose the operation.

Eduardo has earned $8.50 doing chores this week. Jacob has earned $9.45. How much have they earned altogether?

subtraction
Ⓐ

division
Ⓑ

addition
Ⓒ

multiplication
Ⓓ

28. Alexa found 5 beautiful rocks during a camping trip. She found 4 more on the side of the hill near the campsite. Her dad wants her to bring home a total of 20 rocks. How many more rocks does she need to find?

11
Ⓕ

9
Ⓖ

6
Ⓗ

24
Ⓙ

29. Identify the unnecessary information.

Apples sell for $.49 per pound. Oranges sell for $.89 per pound. Anthony needs 4 pounds of apples. How much will he pay?

Ⓐ Apples sell for $.49 per pound.

Ⓑ Oranges sell for $.89 per pound.

Ⓒ Anthony needs 4 pounds of apples.

Ⓓ NG

30. The fish store is adding new fish to the aquarium every day. There are 14 fish in the aquarium today. Yesterday, there were 12. The day before that, there were 10. If the pattern was the same, how many were there in the aquarium 3 days before there were 10?

0 fish
Ⓕ

4 fish
Ⓖ

8 fish
Ⓗ

2 fish
Ⓙ

GO ON

Final Review Test

Draw 6 lines. Two lines should
be parallel and 2 lines should
be perpendicular.

Tell why the lines are parallel and perpendicular.

_____

_____

_____

_____

Answer Key

Page 5

1. 16; 2. 16; 3. 9; 4. 6; 5. 6; 6. 5; 7. 3; 8. 17; 9. 15; 10. 7; 11. 13; 12. 17; 13. 13; 14. 15; 15. 12; 16. 17; 17. 15; 18. 12; 19. 14; 20. 15; 21. 16; 22. 5; 23. 12; 24. 6; 25. 7; 26. 5

Page 6

A. >, >, <; B. <, >, =; C. >, <, >; D. >, =, <; E. <, >, <; F. =, >, >; G. >, <; H. >, <; I. >, <

Page 7

Ten: 70; 10; 80; 50; 60; 60; 20; 30; 30; 100; 70; 40; Hundred: 300; 600; 800; 700; 900; 400; 700; 200; 800; 400; Greatest Number: 20,000; 70,000; 600,000; 4,000; 6,000; 8,000; 10,000; 4,000; 6,000; 40,000; 30,000; 6,000,000

Page 8

1. 93; 2. 86; 3. 133; 4. 97; 5. 132; 6. 722; 7. 615; 8. 807; 9. 860; 10. 681; 11. 679; 12. 1,026; 13. 1,166; 14. 1,093; 15. 1,056; MATH IS A BLAST!

Page 9

1. 8,730; 2. 7,821; 3. 10,623; 4. 4,415; 5. 64,802; 6. 5,546; 7. 46,073; 8. 43,563; 9. 58,621; 10. 96,442; 11. 62,343; 12. 73,332; 13. 81,530; 14. 106,008; 15. 351,474; 16. 693,477

Page 10

1. 258; 2. 256; 3. 126; 4. 264; 5. 177; 6. 488; 7. 758; 8. 3,596; 9. 3,757; 10. 1,463; 11. 8,918; 12. 1,886; 13. 1,689; 14. 1,778; 15. 1,889; 16. 3,856

Page 11

1. 1,746; 2. 4,368; 3. 5,878; 4. 3,936; 5. 77,827; 6. 88,658; 7. 6,069; 8. 37,789; 9. 19,103; 10. 32,997; 11. 5,658; 12. 33,248; 13. 17,745; 14. 18,878; 15. 46,383; 16. 92,814

Page 12

1. 366; 2. 401; 3. 122; 4. 576; 5. 173; 6. 244; 7. 1,764; 8. 2,047; 9. 6,722; 10. 519; 11. 2,853; 12. 8,719; 13. 4,109; 14. 2,916; 15. 7,884; 16. 3,393

Page 13

1. $1.43; 2. $8.27; 3. $70.61; 4. $.56; 5. $.93; 6. $19.17; 7. $604.07; 8. $573.71; 9. $361.00; 10. $171.05; 11. $270.42; 12. $377.11; A NEW BICYCLE!

Unit 1 Test

1. B; 2. A; 3. B; 4. C; 5. A; 6. B; 7. D; 8. D; 9. A; 10. C; 11. C; 12. A; 13. C; 14. B; 15. B; 16. D; 17. A; 18. B; 19. A; 20. B; Constructed-response answers will vary.

Page 18

1. 18, 32, 0, 45, 21; 2. 28, 36, 10, 72, 24; 3. 24, 12, 33, 36, 36; 4. 14, 22, 25, 56, 66; 5. 0, 16, 42, 49, 96; 8, 4, 2, 10; 2, 2, 10, 2, 10; 10, 2, 4, 2, 1; 10, 2, 10

Page 19

1. 69; 2. 96; 3. 84; 4. 70; 5. 90; 6. 189; 7. 276; 8. 246; 9. 248; 10. 810; 11. 434; 12. 160; 13. 280; 14. 141; 15. 190; 16. 150; 17. 207; 18. 138; 19. 256; 20. 261

Page 20

1. 642; 2. 568; 3. 2,550; 4. 972; 5. 1,048; 6. 738; 7. 2,056; 8. 1,491; 9. 3,708; 10. 2,526; 11. 1,770; 12. 1,008; 13. 2,448; 14. 711; 15. 2,172

Page 21

1. 9,369; 2. 8,486; 3. 25,926; 4. 4,912; 5. 11,008; 6. 22,615; 7. 16,926; 8. 25,281; 9. 30,834; 10. 14,061; 11. 18,512; 12. 32,291

Page 22

1. 1,800; 2. 2,800; 3. 4,000; 4. 480; 5. 200; 6. 1,800; 7. 240; 8. 240; 9. 32,000; 10. 42,000; 11. 3,200; 12. 12,000; 13. 48,000; 14. 9,600; 15. 200; 16. 1,200; 17. 1,600; 18. 7,000; 19. 8,000; 20. 8,000

Page 23

1. 672; 2. 924; 3. 1,026; 4. 2,736; 5. 1,219; 6. 1,035; 7. 1,525; 8. 1,316; 9. 532; 10. 2,346; 11. 2,592; 12. 1,066; 13. 1,372; 14. 1,246

Page 24

1. 7,440; 2. 14,420; 3. 10,136; 4. 17,220; 5. 12,489; 6. 12,546; 7. 7,955; 8. 26,244; 9. 16,848; 10. 28,764; 11. 12,705; 12. 9,614

Page 25

1. $55.43; 2. $23.34; 3. $7.14; 4. $192.96; 5. $26.04; 6. $46.23; 7. $314.50; 8. $37.74; 9. $10.29; 10. $29.47; 11. $45.36; 12. $136.64; 13. $89.04; 14. $11.96

Page 26

Guesses will vary: 1. $20.46, $18; 2. $9.84, $8; 3. $78.96, $80; 4. $98.49, $100; 5. $170.50; 6. $40.80; 7. $99.28

Unit 2 Test

1. A; 2. B; 3. D; 4. C; 5. A; 6. B; 7. C; 8. A; 9. B; 10. D; 11. C; 12. D; 13. C; 14. B; 15. C; 16. C; 17. A; 18. B; 19. D; 20. A; Constructed-response answers will vary.

Page 31

1. 5 R2; 2. 8 R1; 3. 4 R1; 4. 3 R2; 5. 4 R3; 6. 9 R3; 7. 6 R3; 8. 2 R4; 9. 9 R3; 10. 3 R3; 11. 5 R5; 12. 8 R3; 13. 3 R4; 14. 5 R5; 15. 6 R2; 16. 5 R2; 17. 2 R3; 18. 5 R4; 19. 5 R3; 20. 9 R3

Page 32

1. 21; 2. 32; 3. 21; 4. 34; 5. 13; 6. 18; 7. 25; 8. 13; 9. 17; 10. 12; 11. 16; 12. 28; 13. 19; 14. 12; 15. 12; 16. 38

Page 33

1. 13 R2; 2. 11 R4; 3. 35 R1; 4. 11 R3; 5. 22 R3; 6. 22 R1; 7. 46 R1; 8. 15 R2; 9. 12 R2; 10. 13 R1; 11. 15 R4; 12. 13 R4; 13. 23 R3; 14. 14 R2; 15. 11 R3

Answer Key

Page 34

1. 145; 2. 137; 3. 129; 4. 472;
5. 123; 6. 136; 7. 314; 8. 218;
9. 125; 10. 178; 11. 135; 12. 259;
13. 138; 14. 147; 15. 178

Page 35

1. 178 R2; 2. 145 R3; 3. 218 R2;
4. 128 R3; 5. 347 R1; 6. 169 R2;
7. 259 R2; 8. 482 R1; 9. 99 R2;
10. 126 R4; 11. 134 R3; 12. 152 R4;
13. 125 R4; 14. 387 R1; 15. 117 R4

Page 36

1. 308 R1; 2. 180 R4; 3. 406 R1;
4. 209 R3; 5. 140 R5; 6. 109 R2;
7. 120 R6; 8. 108 R2; 9. 340;
10. 190; 11. 405 R1; 12. 103 R4;
13. 140 R5; 14. 207 R1; 15. 106 R5

Page 37

1. 813; 2. 3,212; 3. 984; 4. 1,258;
5. 867; 6. 640; 7. 852; 8. 495;
9. 547; 10. 526; 11. 198; 12. 1,245

Page 38

1. 428 R2; 2. 3,421 R1; 3. 284 R3;
4. 216 R3; 5. 412 R3; 6. 634 R4; 7.
385 R3; 8. 3,122 R1; 9. 452 R2; 10.
247 R1; 11. 4,234 R1; 12. 467 R4

Page 39

1. $3.24; 2. $3.23; 3. $1.27;
4. $1.14; 5. $2.16; 6. $2.18; 7.
$1.13; 8. $2.36; 9. $1.08; 10. $1.24;
11. $2.19; 12. $1.84

Page 40

1. 3 R3; 2. 4 R2; 3. 5 R10; 4. 9 R7;
5. 8 R4; 6. 3 R43; 7. 6 R10; 8. 8 R20;
9. 4 R4; 10. 8 R12; 11. 4 R26; 12. 5
R9; 13. 1 R80; 14. 7 R20; 15. 5 R10

Unit 3 Test

1. B; 2. C; 3. C; 4. B; 5. A; 6. C; 7. C;
8. B; 9. D; 10. A; 11. C; 12. C; 13. B;
14. D; 15. A; 16. C; 17. A; 18. C; 19.
D; 20. B; Constructed-response
answers will vary.

Page 45

1. 4/10, 0.4; 2. 2/10, 0.2; 3. 5/10,
0.5; 4. 1 4/10, 1.4; 5. 1 1/10, 1.1; 6.
2 9/10, 2.9

Page 46

1. 21/100, 0.21; 2. 47/100, 0.47;
3. 34/100, 0.34; 4. 69/100, 0.69;
5. 1 7/100, 1.07; 6. 1 2/100, 1.02;
7. 2 4/100, 2.04; 8. 1/100, 0.01

Page 47

1. >; 2. <; 3. >; 4. <; 5. <; 6. <; 7. >; 8.
>; 9. >; 10. >; 11. <; 12. >; 13. <; 14.
<; 15. <; 16. <; 17. >; 18. >; 19. >;
20. <

Page 48

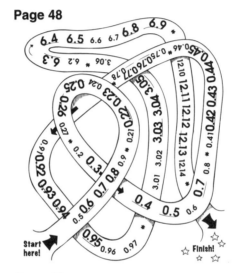

Page 49

1. 4, 7, 11, 6; 2. 21, 11, 5, 14; 3. 9,
8, 9, 11; 4. 10, 10, 8, 7; 5. 6.3, 10.7,
14.8, 6.8; 6. 3.5, 24.4, 17.5, 28.2; 7.
5.5, 10.4, 3.6, 6.3; 8. 17.6, 112.3,
9.4, 400.7; 4U!

Page 50

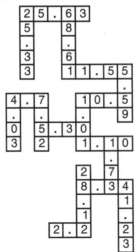

Page 51

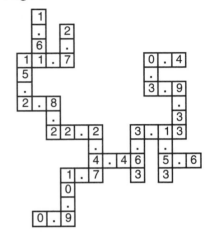

Page 52

1. 2.3; 2. 1.2; 3. 0.64; 4. 6.2; 5. 2.4;
6. 5.6; 7. 3.18; 8. 2.74; 9. 0.83;
10. 7.6; 11. 3.02; 12. 3.87; 13.
13.16; 14. 4.46; 15. 1.1; 16. 3.36;
17. 3.37; 18. 4.36; 19. 7.2; 20.
20.86; A. 0.6; B. 3.05; C. 3.54; D.
6.75; E. 11.12

Unit 4 Test

1. A; 2. C; 3. B; 4. B; 5. D; 6. A; 7. D;
8. A; 9. B; 10. C; 11. B; 12. C; 13. D;
14. B; 15. A; 16. B; 17. C; 18. C;
19. C; 20. B; Constructed response:
1. Monday: 4 lbs., Tuesday: 6 lbs.,
Wednesday: 7 lbs.; 2. 2.3 extra
tenths; 3. $9.20; Written answers
will vary.

Midway Review Test

1. C; 2. F; 3. D; 4. G; 5. D; 6. F; 7. C;
8. G; 9. D; 10. G; 11. C; 12. G; 13. A;
14. G; 15. C; 16. F; 17. C; 18. F;
19. B; 20. F; 21. D; 22. G; 23. B;
24. F; 25. C; Constructed-response
answers will vary.

Page 63

1. ray CD; 2. line CM; 3. line
segment XY; 4. line AB; 5. line
segment BC; 6. line ST; 7. ray EF;
8. ray DE; 9. intersecting lines;
10. parallel lines; 11. perpendicular
lines; 12. parallel lines

Answer Key

Page 64
1. acute; 2. right; 3. obtuse; 4. right; 5. obtuse; 6. acute; 7. obtuse; 8. right; 9. acute; 10. obtuse

Page 65
1. (1,1); 2. (8, 3); 3. (3, 4); 4. (3, 1); 5. (4, 5); 6. (6, 3); 7. (7, 1); 8. (4, 2); 9. (1, 3); 10. (7, 4); MATH HELPS YOU GET THE POINT!

Page 66
yes; no

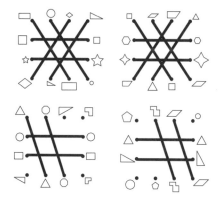

Page 67
1. quadrilateral; 2. triangle; 3. triangle; 4. pentagon; 5. quadrilateral; 6. triangle; 7. pentagon; 8. pentagon; 9. quadrilateral; 10. triangle; 11. quadrilateral; 12. pentagon; 13. square; 14. parallelogram; 15. rectangle; 16. parallelogram

Page 68
1. 14; 2. 11; 3. 10; 4. 9; 5. 11; 6. 16; 7. 18; 8. 24; 9. 24; 10. 40; 11. 10; 12. 50; 13. 15; 14. 72

Page 69
1. 6; 2. 48; 3. 9; 4. 1; 5. 16; 6. 20; 7. 36; 8. 6; 9. 12; 10. 40; 11. 64; 12. 8; 21, 108, 64, 648, 841

Page 70
1. pyramid; 2. cylinder; 3. sphere; 4. cone; 5. cube; 6. rectangular prism; 7. pyramid; 8. sphere; 9. cylinder; 10. pyramid; 11. cube; 12. cube; 13. cone; 14. cylinder; 15. sphere; 16. cylinder

Page 71
1. yes; 2. yes; 3. yes; 4. no; 5. yes; 6. yes; 7. no; 8. no; 9. yes; 10. no; 11. yes; 12. yes; 13. yes; 14. yes; 15. no;

More than one line of symmetry may be correct. Check that students have at least one correct choice.

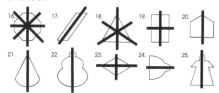

Unit 5 Test
1. C; 2. A; 3. B; 4. B; 5. B; 6. B; 7. D; 8. B; 9. B; 10. A; 11. C; 12. B; 13. B; 14. A; 15. C; 16. A; 17. B; 18. C; 19. D; 20. A; Constructed-response answers will vary.

Page 76
1. 4/6; 2. 1/3; 3. 2/3; 4. 1/4; 5. 1/3; 6. 2/4; 7. 3/6; 8. 3/8; 9. 2/4; 10. 1/2; 11. 1/4; 12. 2/6; 13. 3/4; 14. 6/12; 15. 5/15; 16. 4/5; 17. 3/9; 18. 1/6; 19. 4/7; 20. 2/5

Page 77
1. 5; 2. 2; 3. 5; 4. 5; 5. 2; 6. 3; 7. 4; 8. 9; 9. 6; 10. 5; 11. 9; 12. 4; 13. 9; 14. 14; 15. 8; 16. 2; 17. 4; 18. 9; 19. 8; 20. 15

Page 78
1. 1/3 = 2/6; 2. 1/4 = 2/8; 3. 1/2 = 3/6; 4. 3/4 = 6/8; 5. 2/2 = 1/1; 6. 3/7 = 6/14; 7. 1/5 = 2/10; 8. 1/6 = 2/12; 9. 8/8 = 1/1; 10. 2/3 = 6/9; 11. 2/4 = 8/16; 12. 1/4 = 3/12; 13. 1/3 = 2/6; 14. 2/3 = 4/6; 15. 1/2 = 5/10

Page 79
1. 5/6; 2. 1/4; 3. 1/3; 4. 2/3; 5. 7/8; 6. 1/3; 7. 1/3; 8. 2/5; 9. 1/2; 10. 1/3; 11. 1/2; 12. 5/8; 13. 1/2; 14. 1/2; 15. 6/7; 16. 4/5; 17. 1/4; 18. 1/3; 19. 1/4; 20. 1/5; 21. 1/4

Page 80
1. 2 1/7; 2. 3 1/2; 3. 2 1/3; 4. 2 1/5; 5. 1 8/9; 6. 3 1/4; 7. 3 1/5; 8. 5 1/2; 9. 2 1/2; 10. 4 1/5; 11. 3 5/6; 12. 3 1/6; 13. 4 1/2; 14. 2 1/2; 15. 4 1/3; 16. 2 1/4; 17. 1 2/7; 18. 7 1/2; 19. 2 4/5; 20. 1 5/8; 21. 2 1/6

Page 81
1. 5/7; 2. 7/9; 3. 9/14; 4. 3/5; 5. 9/11; 6. 3/4; 7. 1 2/5; 8. 7/9; 9. 1 1/2; 10. 10/13; 11. 7/8; 12. 4/5; 13. 1 1/10; 14. 7/11; 15. 8/9; 16. 1 1/4; 17. 9/10; 18. 5/6

Page 82
1. 1/4; 2. 2/7; 3. 1/10; 4. 3/11; 5. 1/3; 6. 1/4; 7. 2/13; 8. 2/9; 9. 1/5; 10. 2/9; 11. 1/6; 12. 2/7; 13. 2/5; 14. 2/3; 15. 5/14; 16. 5/11; 17. 7/17; 18. 5/13

Page 83
1. >; 2. <; 3. <; 4. <; 5. <; 6. >; 7. >; 8. >; 9. <; 10. <; 11. >; 12. >; 13. <; 14. <; 15. >; 16. =; 17. >; 18. >; 19. =; 20. >; 21. >

Page 84
1. 3/10; 2. 3/4; 3. 9/14; 4. 11/15; 5. 3/4; 6. 5/6; 7. 7/8; 8. 5/8; 9. 9/14; 10. 1/2; 11. 7/10; 12. 7/12; 13. 9/10; 14. 1/2; 15. 7/9; 16. 1/4; 17. 4/5; 18. 1/2; 19. 1; 20. 7/8

Page 85
1. 1/4; 2. 1/4; 3. 3/10; 4. 3/14; 5. 1/6; 6. 1/4; 7. 3/8; 8. 1/10; 9. 1/6; 10. 1/12; 11. 0; 12. 1/4; 13. 1/4; 14. 1/10; 15. 1/14; 16. 3/8

Unit 6 Test
1. B; 2. C; 3. B; 4. A; 5. B; 6. A; 7. D; 8. B; 9. B; 10. C; 11. A; 12. B; 13. A; 14. D; 15. C; 16. B; 17. A; 18. B; 19. B; 20. A; Constructed-response answers will vary.

Page 90
1. 30, 1; 2. 25, 3; 3. 10, 12; 4. 15, 8; 5. 55, 5; 5, 6; 6. 40, 1; 20, 2; 7. 45, 10; 15, 11; 8. 6:10; 9. 7:35; 10. 9:40; 11. 5:10

Answer Key

Page 91

1. Thursday; 2. 4th; 3. 4; 4. Monday, March 19th; 5. Saturday, March 31st; 6. Thursday; 7. 27th; 8. Wednesday; 9. Friday; 10. 31st; 11. 2; 12. 15th; 13. Wednesday, July 25th; 14. 14th

Page 92

1. B; 2. C; 3. A; 4. C; 5. C; 6. B; 7. A; 8. B; 9. A; 10. A

Page 93

1. g; 2. kg; 3. g; 4. g; 5. kg; 6. g; 7. g; 8. 60 kg; 9. 11 g; 10. 1 kg; 11. 15 kg; 12. 30 g; 13. 10 g; 14. 7 kg

Page 94

1. 5,000; 2. 3,000; 3. 8,000; 4. 1,000; 5. 7,000; 6. 9,000; 7. 2,000; 8. 11,000; 9. 500 mL; 10. 20 mL; 11. 1,000 L; 12. 15 mL; 13. 120 L; 14. 4 L; 15. 5 mL; 16. 80,000 L; 17. 400 mL; 18. 255 mL; 19. 17 mL; 20. 10 mL

Page 95

1. 2 1/2; 2. 3 1/2; 3. 2; 4. 1/2; 5. 3; 6. 5 1/2; 7. 36; 8. 9; 9. 3,520; 10. 120; 11. 21,120; 12. 15; 13. 96; 14. 84; 15. 30; 16. 5,280; 17. 6; 18. 18; 19. in.; 20. yd.; 21. in.; 22. mi.; 23. yd.; 24. yd.; 25. in.; 26. yd.

Page 96

1. <; 2. >; 3. >; 4. =; 5. <; 6. >; 7. >; 8. =; 9. =; 10. <; 11. <; 12. >; 13. <; 14. >; 15. <; 16. oz.; 17. t.; 18. gal.; 19. oz.; 20. c.; 21. gal.; 22. lb.; 23. gal.; 24. 48; 25. 4,000; 26. 8; 27. 4; 28. 6; 29. 6; 30. 80; 31. 10; 32. 32

Page 97

1. 75; 2. 40; 3. 195; 4. 100; 5. 80; 6. 100; 7. 0; 8. 50; 9. 25; 10. 85; 11. E, J; 12. C, F; 13. B, D; 14. G, I; 15. A, H

Page 98

1. fourth; 2. fifth; 3. 3,100 lbs.; 4. 500 lbs.; 5. sixth; 6. 100; 7. sixth; 8. June; 9. 20; 10. April; 11. 20; 12. 160; 13. Sept.; 14. 60

Page 99

1. beets, peas; 2. broccoli; 3. yellow squash; 4. tomatoes; 5. broccoli; 6. yellow squash; 7. broccoli; 8. Dec.; 9. Feb., Mar.; 10. Nov., Dec.; 11. 20; 12. Oct., Mar.; 13. 44

Unit 7 Test

1. B; 2. A; 3. D; 4. A; 5. C; 6. C; 7. B; 8. D; 9. B; 10. C; 11. B; 12. B; 13. D; 14. B; 15. C; 16. A; 17. B; 18. B; 19. C; 20. D; Constructed-response answers will vary.

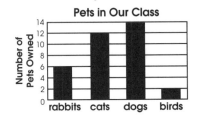

Page 104

1. +, 12; 2. −, 11; 3. ÷, 40; 4. x, 15; 5. +, 49; 6. x, 42

Page 105

1. 9; 2. 10; 3. 10; 4. 4; 5. 25

Page 106

1. yes; 2. $8.97; 3. $8.47; 4. strawberries and bananas; 5. grapes; 6. $1.48; 7. no

Page 107

1. 12 balloons; 2. 19 cans and boxes of food; 3. 150 apples; 4. $6.00; 5. 5 more times; 6. 5 drawings

Page 108

1. 22 students; 2. 89 pounds of paper; 3. $4.41; 4. 44 mice; 5. 65 students

Page 109

1. 216; 2. 84; 3. 467; 4. 100; 5. 783; 6. 92

Page 110

1. Thursday = 18 problems, Friday = 23 problems; 2. 7 bottles of water; 3. 29 gifts; 4. 7 minutes 10 seconds; 5. 27 students; 6. 10 days; 7. 5 dates

Page 111

1. All, All, No; 2. Some, All, No; 3. All, No, Some; 4. Some, All, No; 5. No, Some, All; 6. None; 7. Some; 8. All

Unit 8 Test

1. A; 2. C; 3. D; 4. C; 5. B; 6. A; 7. C; 8. B; 9. B; 10. C; 11. A; 12. B; 13. A; 14. C; 15. D; 16. C; 17. A; 18. D; 19. B; 20. A; Constructed response: 12 choices. Check students' tree diagrams. Answers to questions will vary.

Final Review Test

1. B; 2. H; 3. D; 4. H; 5. A; 6. H; 7. A; 8. J; 9. B; 10. H; 11. D; 12. J; 13. B; 14. H; 15. C; 16. F; 17. B; 18. G; 19. C; 20. G; 21. B; 22. F; 23. B; 24. G; 25. A; 26. G; 27. C; 28. F; 29. B; 30. G; Constructed-response answers will vary.